TOSS KEEP SELL!

The *Suddenly Frugal Guide*
to Cleaning Out the Clutter and Cashing In

LEAH INGRAM
Founder, SuddenlyFrugal.com

Aadamsmedia
Avon, Massachusetts

Published by
Adams Media, a division of F+W Media, Inc.
57 Littlefield Street, Avon, MA 02322. U.S.A.
www.adamsmedia.com

ISBN 10: 1-4405-0598-5
ISBN 13: 978-1-4405-0598-0
eISBN 10: 1-4405-0918-2
eISBN 13: 978-1-4405-0918-6

Printed in the United States of America.

10 9 8 7 6 5 4 3 2

Library of Congress Cataloging-in-Publication Data
Ingram, Leah.
Toss, keep, sell! / Leah Ingram.
p. cm.
ISBN 978-1-4405-0598-0
1. Storage in the home. 2. House cleaning. 3. Secondhand trade. I. Title.
TX309.I527 2010
648'.5—dc22
2010038853

Recycling icons © iStockphoto/kathykonkle
Money icons © iStockphoto/browndogstudios

This book is available at quantity discounts for bulk purchases.
For information, please call 1-800-289-0963.

CONTENTS

ACKNOWLEDGMENTS

Hillary Rodham Clinton may have famously said that it takes a village to raise a child, but I firmly believe that it takes a village to write a book. With this latest book in mind, that saying was as true as ever.

First, a shout out to all of my friends (virtual and real life) with whom I communicate on Facebook and Twitter as well as an online community for writers called Freelance Success (*www.freelancesuccess.com*). When I put out a call online for anecdotes on how people made cash from their clutter, these folks responded in droves.

Similarly, I wouldn't have been able to find the breadth of people that I interviewed for this book—beyond my friends—without two Internet resources that help writers like me find information for the pieces they're writing, whether that piece be a magazine article, a TV segment or a book. Those resources are Profnet (*www.profnet.com*) and Help a Reporter Out or HARO (*www.helpareporter.com*).

Thanks also to Jami Osiecki, a producer for the *10! Show* at NBC 10 in Philadelphia. For the past year she's been receptive to nearly every frugal segment idea I've pitched her, and as a result I've been a guest expert on the show about once a month. Many of these ideas that I ended up discussing on the show were those I was working on when researching and writing *Toss, Keep, Sell!* and had I not had the opportunity to bring them to life on TV, I might not have found them valid enough to include in this book.

My literary agent Adam Chromy of Artists and Artisans got me to brainstorm the idea for this book, and my husband and children help me to put the book's premise into action by working to declutter our house and get money for doing so. If it hadn't worked for us, it never would have worked for the people I hope will buy this book, and I couldn't have included any of this advice in good conscience. But trust me, people, you really can get cash for your clutter, and I hope that in reading this book you'll end up with a neater home and more money in your pocket.

Introduction

GETTING ORGANIZED DOESN'T HAVE TO COST A LOT

Would you like to start making money by selling your old clothes and your clutter? There's no reason to pay anywhere from $50 to $100 an hour to hire a professional organizer to go through your closets—you can do that yourself. A professional is also likely to recommend fancy storage and organizational systems to get your house in order, but I'll bet that you probably already own all you need to get neat and tidy. I believe you can do it all yourself.

Businesses that profit from people's clutter would say that you need their help. After all, with American households more cluttered than ever, their revenue is on the rise. The company 1-800-GOT-JUNK has hauled away more than five million truck-loads since its founding in 1989. There are more than 7,000 "I Sold It" franchises nationwide that help people make money from their clutter by selling it on eBay (for a fee). And self-storage facilities are popping up all across the country. The National Association of Resale and Thrift Shops reports that business at resale and consignment shops is booming. For example, Buffalo Exchange consignment chain expects revenues to rise from $56.3 million in 2009 to $70 million by 2015.

That's where this book comes in. It will help frugal folks like you get your home in order and help you find ways to make money from things you no longer need or want.

A recent survey on my blog Suddenly Frugal (*www.suddenly frugal.com*) showed that there is a tremendous interest in making money while getting more organized. For example, 92 percent of survey takers have sold their clutter for cash and would do so again in the future. Many of the people who took this survey have used more than one selling method to sell various household items.

Here are some highlights from that survey:

(Note: Because people may have used more than one way to get cash for their trash, they likely marked multiple answers for the survey question "What method do you use to sell your stuff?" This is why the numbers below add up to more than 100 percent.)

- O   74% hold yard sales to get rid of excess stuff

- O   51% use Craigslist to get cash for clutter

- O   48% rely on eBay to sell off their stuff

- O   40% take their castoffs to a consignment or resale shop

○ 20% find other ways to make money from their stuff, ranging from classified ads to neighborhood listservs to Amazon's Marketplace to local flea markets

When trying to get cash for things they no longer need, here's what people who took this survey were selling the most often:

○ Books (77%)

○ Clothing (72%)

○ Furniture (71%)

○ Games and toys (61%)

○ Appliances (35%)

○ Jewelry and accessories (33% each)

○ Other "stuff," including sporting equipment, collectibles, and electronics (38%)

People seem to do fairly well in making money from their things. In most instances, survey takers make a couple hundred dollars from items they might have just thrown out!

Of those items making money, here are the two things that sell the best:

○ Furniture (43%)

○ Clothing (19%)

One person added a comment to the survey that she'd made nearly $3,000 from selling her old furniture. Wow!

While I'll be sure to include some tried-and-true methods for selling your stuff and making money from it, I'm also going to offer you options that you may not have heard of or considered, but that will put cash in your pocket, in one way or another.

For example, in that aforementioned survey, people reported that while they sold books often (77% of the time), they didn't make much money from them. This is why, in addition to giving you inside tips in this book on selling your clutter for cash, I've added a "bonus" chapter on swapping—that is, swapping stuff, not spouses. (See Chapter 11, Getting What You Want by Swapping or Trading.) I, too, have found that I "make" more money from used books by trading them for other used books rather than trying to sell them for greenbacks—or more likely, because they sell so poorly, only spare change.

Sure, I want you to find a way to make money from your clutter but I also want this book to help you clear out your excess stuff and love living in your home again. I've been there, and I know how it feels to have someone drop by unexpectedly, only to end up running around and closing off the rooms in a disaster state before you answer the front door. Because clutter usually isn't limited to a single spot in the house, I've organized this book so that the chapters go room to room. I've suggested tasks you can do slowly—but surely—to get your house, life, and "stuff" in control over time.

Because I know firsthand how overwhelming it can be to take back control of a home, I've taken to heart a mantra I once heard: "You can do anything in fifteen minutes." True, you may not get everything *done* or finished or put away in fifteen minutes, but you can make a pretty significant dent in a project in just that short period of time. It's how I get through my daily life, and I'm sure it'll help you get through yours.

That's why in each chapter of this book you'll find at least one "Quick Clutter Challenge." You'll set your timer for fifteen minutes, and I'll challenge you to collect a certain kind of clutter. The idea is not only to neaten up the place, but the items you'll be looking for are ones that you can sell in the near future or that can save you money in the long run.

You'll also find a chart called "Toss, Keep, Sell" in each chapter. Each chart includes items mentioned in that chapter that you should toss, recycle, keep, sell, or swap. This will help you differentiate between the clutter that might be worth saving because it could have monetary value; the clutter that's worth keeping around for sentimental, decorating, or daily use; and the clutter that you would be better off putting in the trash can or recycling bin.

Keep in mind that in some chapters, you may see items in the "Toss, Keep, Sell" chart that I mention in other chapters. For instance, I have reading material in multiple rooms of my house—part of my clutter problem. So for the book's purpose, you'll notice that in Chapter 2 (about the family room) and Chapter 9 (about the home office), the "Toss, Keep, Sell" charts both address what to do with magazines. The more you read these "Toss, Keep, Sell" messages, the more likely you are to act on them.

You will also get an inside look at real-life people who've sold their clutter for cash. Throughout the book you'll find "Cashing In" elements. These are mini-profiles of folks who found themselves living in disorganized homes with too much stuff and no idea what to do with it—until one day they figured out that they could make some extra money while clearing out their closets, cupboards, and cabinets. Within these profiles you'll find tips you can use to get out from under your own clutter and start cashing in, too. "Cashing In" will offer helpful advice on what selling method to use (Craigslist versus a consignment shop, for example), how to price your items, and what you can do to increase the chances that you'll get the most money possible for your things. (Hint: Dirty stuff usually sells for 50 percent less than the pieces you took the time to clean up, dust off, or shine up.)

Another regular feature in this book are "What's It Worth?". These are stories that highlight treasures that someone mistook for trash, and interviews with an antiques expert or auctioneer. Some of these stories come with an eye-popping price tag attached! Through anecdotes and expert advice you should have a better sense about whether or not something you own—like grandma's china set or that painting that's been hanging in your living room forever—is valuable enough that you ought to arrange to bring it to your local auction house rather than your local junk shop.

Finally, I've quantified my clutter-busting and money-saving advice by ending each chapter with a section titled "Total Cash Back in This Chapter." Here, I'll briefly recount some of the advice from the chapter, especially if it had a price tag attached to it. Then, I'll add up all the cash you could potentially have saved or gotten back from following my advice. This should inspire dollar signs in your eyes—and real cash in your wallet—along with a neater space in which to live and work.

chapter 1

ORGANIZATION TOOLS YOU PROBABLY ALREADY OWN

There's something absolutely refreshing about deciding that you're finally going to get yourself organized, and then something absolutely defeating when you discover how much it can cost to get organized. If you've considered hiring a professional organizer, expect to pay between $55 and $85 an hour. Since most organizers want a four-hour minimum for a booking, you'll be committed to spending $220 to $340.

Maybe you'll decide to skip hiring a professional organizer (wise) for something I'm confident you can do yourself, and stock up on organizing products at the store instead (not so wise), because you've seen how they come color coordinated and with the name of your favorite magazine or celebrity on them. While pretty, these are pricey, too. For example, a *Real Simple* magazine–branded organizational tote, in robin's egg blue, sells at Target for $30. An expanding file folder system in the same pretty blue from the same product line costs $14. If you were really stuck on buying something new to start your organizing, you could get a similar tote or no-name expanding file at an office supply store for half the price.

Hey, I'm all for brand loyalty when you know a product works. Maybe if someone is looking to buy you a gift on your next birthday, you can tell that person that one of these beautiful organizational tools would be a perfect present.

But the rest of us have to make do with what we've got. That's why this chapter focuses on getting organized using stuff you likely already own. That's the frugal thing to do, because if you already own it, you don't have to go out and buy something new. This saves you money in the long run. So read on for how you can make everything from unwanted gifts to empty shoeboxes into organizational products that work for you.

The Three Rs of Home Organization

Getting your home organized on a budget isn't about reading, writing, and 'rithmetic—although there is a little math involved in there. Rather, it is all about reducing, reusing, and recycling: reducing what you currently own; reusing items you already own; and recycling (or selling off, giving away, or throwing out) things you're no longer interested in owning.

REDUCING

Take the first step to tackling clutter in your house by asking yourself these questions:

1. Do I love this item?

2. Do I use this item on a regular basis?

3. Do I foresee myself using this item in the near future?

4. Is this an item I feel like I *should* keep and therefore it's just taking up space and giving me one more thing to dust?

Clearly, if you answered "yes" to the first three questions, then you should keep the item. But if you at all hesitated in answering "yes" to questions two and three, then I'm thinking the time has come to get rid of the item in question. And that is also what I would suggest you do if you answered "yes" to question number four—think about getting rid of that space-hogging, dust-collecting item.

Let me address items that likely come to mind when asking yourself question number four. In all my years of giving gift and etiquette advice (on my website: *www.giftsandetiquette.com*), I hear repeatedly from people who have received gifts that they don't love, never wanted, can't use, and didn't return. However, because these people received this gift for an important occasion (graduation, wedding, child's birth), they feel that they have to keep that item around because of assumed sentimentality.

I know that I used to feel this way, especially soon after I got married. My friends and family were very generous with gifts for my husband and me. However, every time any of our former wedding guests came over to visit, I felt like I needed to find the gift they'd given to us and either put it out on display or use it somehow during their visit, because I wanted to *make them happy*. But what about my happiness?

What kind of crazy stress was I causing myself with this pre-entertaining running around and rummaging in closets to find the cake server that my husband's aunt's second cousin gave to me at my bridal shower?

It finally dawned on me one day, after I'd collapsed in tears when I realized I couldn't remember what gift a visiting relative had given to me—and therefore I couldn't bring it out for her visit—that maybe she doesn't even remember what gift she gave me. And she probably isn't even expecting to see the gift during her visit—I know that I never make such assumptions when I visit someone to whom *I've* given a gift. Would it make me happy to see the gift in use? Sure—if I actually remembered what I gave the person. But the bottom line with gifts is this: Once the gift leaves your hands, it is out of your control. You cannot suggest what the recipient should do with your gift once she takes possession of it. Why I couldn't remember my own advice is beyond me.

Nonetheless, what really drove the message home—that this displaying-of-the-wedding-gifts ritual was unnecessary—was what happened one time when I'd gone through my pre-visit ritual. I'd found what I'd thought someone had given me for my wedding, brought it out during her visit, and then *commented* on it. Guess what? The person hadn't given me the hand-painted salad bowl from Italy that I'd sworn all of these years was her gift. Boy, was I embarrassed.

Never again, I swore, was I going to make myself crazy finding gifts that I didn't love and use all the time—just to make someone else happy. What I needed to concentrate on was making *me* happy, and in my current cluttered state, that meant minimizing what I owned, stored, and kept on display—even if it was a long-ago wedding present.

REUSING

Before you go crazy like I did and chuck all those gifts that you've kept around for years, just in case, let's think about something: Is there a way that you can reuse those items so that they double as a storage device or find new life with a secondary purpose?

For example, one of those guilt-laden gifts that I'd alluded to earlier was a small, crystal decanter from Tiffany & Co. that a friend of mine had given me for my wedding. It's a beautiful piece, which probably set her back quite a bit given the pathetic state of the salaries we were earning around the time I got married. I truly appreciated that she wanted to give me such a lovely gift. It was probably all she could afford at the time, but the decanter itself is so small that it's pretty much useless. For years I looked at it on the shelf in a display cabinet, wishing I could put it to good use. Problem is I'm not a big drinker and I don't have parties often where I'm serving alcohol and need a decanter. Guilt, guilt, guilt, that's all I felt.

Then I realized that just because the decanter was sold as such, that doesn't mean that I have to use it that way. Who's going to judge me if I decide to use that decanter to hold loose change, M&Ms, or pens and pencils? And you know what? The decanter *has* held all of those items, at various times over the years, once I figured out a way I could reuse it for a practical purpose.

Reusing something that you already own not only gives the original item a second life, but it also saves you money. I'll never need to buy another piggy bank, candy dish, or pencil box if I've got a container (albeit a crystal one from Tiffany) that I can use for the same purpose.

I've brought up this reusing idea now, to get the wheels in your brain moving. That's because later in this chapter, I start suggesting ways for you to find organizational tools that you already own and can use to get your house back under control—and you won't have to spend any extra money in the process. You'll even end up *saving* money.

RECYCLING

If I hadn't found a way to reuse that aforementioned Tiffany decanter, I probably would have found a way to recycle it. Since you can't just put crystal in your glass recycle bin, I would have given it away, sold it at a yard sale, or brought it to a thrift, resale, or consignment shop. I no longer wanted or needed it, so if I couldn't figure out an "out of the box" way to use it, I had to get it out of my house. Do the same with anything that you can't justify keeping, or you can't figure out a practical way of reusing. This "recycling" method is sure to make a dent in your clutter—even if it doesn't put cash in your pocket right away.

Twenty-five Ways to Think Outside of the Shoebox for Storage Ideas

Chances are somewhere in your house you've got shoeboxes. Maybe you're using them to hold actual pairs of shoes, or maybe you've put them aside for a diorama project your child will likely have to do in school at some point. Did you ever stop to think about how those shoeboxes could become out-of-the-box home organizers and money-savers for you? I thought of twenty-five ways to reuse them:

1. Bring cookies to a bake sale

2. Organize family photos that didn't make it into an album (label by year, kids, or event on the shoebox's top)

3. Ship something

4. Act as your "cash box" when you have a yard sale

5. Put an oddly shaped gift into it so that you can wrap it more easily

6. Make a mending kit to hold scissors, thread, and needles

7. Create a "mail" box, with note cards and stamps for thank-you note writing

8. Set up a bill-paying center with stamps, return address labels, your checkbook and envelopes, along with unpaid bills

9. Store trial-sized bottles of shampoo, conditioner, lotion, and soap

10. Hold orphaned socks in the laundry room; when the box is full, see how many pairs of socks you can match up

11. Transform into a drawer organizer in the kitchen (use shoebox top only for shallow drawers)

12. Store small holiday decorations

13. Organize CDs and DVDs

14. Make a first-aid kit for your car

15. Create a coupon organizer

16. Make a makeshift jewelry box

17. Craft a ribbon holder and dispenser for when you're wrapping presents

18. Shuffle up a box for card playing, including poker chips

19. Organize a shoeshine kit

20. Turn skinny shoeboxes (like the kind Converse sneakers come in) into holders for taper candles

21. Get your seed packets and other gardening supplies in order

22. Hold rolled coins that you need to take to the bank to cash in

23. Make a travel game kit for the kids to use on car trips

24. Store all the plugs and chargers for electronic devices

25. Organize your writing instruments, with a shoebox each for crayons, markers, pens, pencils, etc.

Twenty-two Totally Tubular Uses for Paper-Towel Rolls or Tubes

In my last book, *Suddenly Frugal*, I suggested ways that you could reuse the cardboard tubes you find inside paper-towel and toilet-paper rolls, but from a "hey, did you know you could use these things for this?" kind of way. But they can also be *de facto* organizers that you can use in at least twenty-two everyday ways.

1. Store bracelets or hang earrings on them, and then neatly stack in a jewelry box

2. Keep computer cords and other electronics' power supplies neat and tidy

3. Hold taper candles

4. Secure small holiday decorations in larger boxes

5. Store plastic bags

6. Encase craft supplies, such as pipe cleaners

7. Unite socks to organize your kids' dresser

8. Hold girls' tights

9. Store women's pantyhose

10. Stash loose ribbon or yarn

11. Stack spools of thread

12. Organize napkin rings

13. Hold cloth napkins

14. Wrap Christmas lights around

15. Hold paintbrushes

16. Keep loose light bulbs

17. Store prescription medication bottles

18. Encase knives

19. Organize hair accessories

20. Hold rolls of wrapping paper

21. Store magazines

22. File kids' paintings and art work

Other Items to Reuse to Get Organized

Clearly, paper towel rolls and shoeboxes aren't the only household items you can reuse for your new organizational system. Some other oldies-but-goodies include coffee cans or containers, and baby-food jars (my husband has them filled with nails, screws, and nuts in his workshop).

Twenty-eight Ideas for How Shoe Holders Can Hold More Than Shoes

What is it about Americans and their shoes? We are forever trying to figure out the best way to store them, whether it be in shoeboxes laden with Polaroid pictures of the contents or those plastic shoe holders that you hang over the back of a door. But what if you already own hanging shoe holders and you don't need them to hold shoes anymore? Here are twenty-eight ways that you can transform a shoe holder into an organization tool for non-footwear items:

1. Make them home sweet home for dolls—one doll per plastic compartment

2. Match and store pairs of socks

3. Hold hats, scarves, and mittens for winter weather

4. Keep coupons organized as you plan your food shopping

5. Create "in boxes" for your mail

6. Make a makeup or hair accessory holder

7. Store toiletries

8. Hold hand towels

9. Keep craft supplies, like spools of ribbon or balls of yarn

10. Hang inside the shower to hold shampoo, razors, and soap

11. Organize small electronics (cell phones, MP3 players, GPS, etc.)

12. Store stuffed animals

13. Keep sample-sized toiletries (like the kind you get at hotels)

14. Hold paperback books

15. Act as a jewelry box

16. Divide snacks in a pantry

17. Organize pet toys

18. Hold nails, screws, and other "fix-it" hardware

19. Act as a vertical spice rack

20. Put it in the car to organize kids' toys and other in-vehicle entertainment

21. Organize gift-wrapping paraphernalia

22. Keep cleaning supplies together

23. Store seed packets and other gardening tools

24. Hold note cards, postage stamps, and return-address labels

25. Collect change

26. Organize magazines and catalogs (roll them up)

27. Keep video games, controllers, and remotes together

28. Design a diaper-changing supply holder

Putting a Decorative Bowl, Plate, or Container to Good Use

When looking to reduce clutter while creating new organizational systems, think outside the china cabinet. Look for decorative items that you use once a year or which you've held on to only for sentimental reasons. I'll use my crystal decanter example again.

As someone who doesn't drink liquor often, I'd never put that decanter to use in its traditional sense. But once I started thinking about it as an organizational product, I found all kinds of ways to use it—as I mentioned earlier, ranging from holding pens and pencils or spare change to being a serving piece for M&Ms at a holiday party.

You may also have decorative bowls, plates, and containers that are doing nothing more than collecting dust in your china cabinet. So, why not consider using them in the following practical ways?

○ For spare change

○ As a place to put your keys

○ An inbox for mail and magazines

○ To lay out jewelry you plan to wear

○ For holding TV remotes

○ As a countertop fruit or vegetable bin

○ To stack daily medications

○ To hold pens, pencils, rulers, and erasers for homework

○ For loose pieces of gum or candy

○ To store sewing or crafting supplies

○ For gift cards

Twenty-four Ways to Get Hooked on Hooks

Many times all it takes to get clutter off the floor is to look up—that is, to use a hanging organizational system rather than piling things all around. It's just like those hanging shoe organizers that you can use to store more than just shoes. You can use hooks in a similar fashion. Maybe you already have hooks in a closet somewhere that you can now use as your free organizational tools. Or, perhaps you have a stash of them in the basement or garage, just waiting to be hung. If so, then get out some screws and your screwdriver. You're about to start hanging hooks around your house so you can use them to hold these twenty-four household items. (Note: If you've got little kids, make sure you hang these hooks low enough to the ground so that the youngest members of your family can use them as much as possible.)

1. Backpacks

2. Hats, gloves, and scarves

3. Lunch boxes

4. Reusable shopping bags

5. Aprons

6. Oven mitts

7. Dog leashes

8. House and car keys

9. Handbags

10. Belts

11. Sweatshirts and coats

12. Shoes (tie the laces together so you can loop them over the hook)

13. Mugs

14. Cooking utensils

15. Pots and pans

16. Extra towels

17. Sports equipment

18. Umbrellas

19. Jewelry, especially necklaces

20. Neckties

21. Extension cords

22. iPod headphones

23. Laundry to dry

24. Pool and beach toys

Fifteen Ways a Childhood Toy Becomes a Real-World Tool

When they don't have the perfect item to fit a need, children often improvise with whatever they can find that does the job. Spoons and pots become drum sets, and towels become capes. I reached for an Altoids Mint not too long ago and found myself remembering how I'd turned a similar tin into a doll suitcase when I was a little girl. Taking a page out of my own book, I began wondering how you might transform an empty Altoids tin into a mini-organizational tool. Not surprisingly I came up with a few ideas.

Here are fifteen ways you can reuse one of these tins to keep your stuff in order—whether in your desk at work, at home, in the car, in your bag, or elsewhere in your daily life:

1. As a makeshift coin purse

2. As a mini sewing kit

3. To hold loose keys

4. As a business card holder

5. As your gift-card wallet

6. To hold tissues

7. To hold nails, screws, nuts, bolts, and washers

8. As a makeshift first-aid kit

9. To hold bobby pins, barrettes, and hair ties

10. To hold birthday candles and matches

11. To store small, handheld video-game cartridges (such as those for Game Boy and Nintendo DS games)

12. As a soap holder when you travel (those free mini bars of soap from hotel rooms would fit perfectly)

13. As a hard-sided case for your small electronics, such as an iPod or digital camera

14. To keep beads and other small crafting supplies

15. As an ear-plug holder

Too Much of a Good Thing

Keep in mind that while it's great to save money by reusing what you own, you should not go overboard with this idea and start hoarding cans, jars, and boxes, just in case you need them one day. Unless no one in your family has any intentions of ever buying shoes again, you will eventually get new shoeboxes that you can reuse to hold stuff. Or, the next time you go food shopping, you may buy a new jar of jam or can of coffee. This means that over time you *will* have a supply of future home-organizing tools. I'd like to see you get your home in order, but not at the risk of creating a fire hazard or ending up such a pack rat that your family has to call an intervention—by the producers of *Hoarders*.

Cashing In
Constance, Minnesota

I have had some experience helping others with estate and garage sales, and I figured I should use some of my expertise to sell my own stuff. I knew I could make money, just not how much, but I also knew that I didn't want to have a lot of loose ends or have to hold onto items for an indefinite amount of time, as you often do when selling on Craigslist or eBay. Instead, I decided to have an estate sale. Basically, I turned my whole house into a room-by-room yard sale.

Initially I started thinking I would just sell the things that were very easy to let go of and that there wouldn't be much to my sale. But as I got into it, I found myself able to let go of more than I realized, and I began putting more and more things in the "to sell" pile.

I started in closets, pulled everything out and sorted stuff based on how long it had been since I used the item and if I saw any need for the item in the near future. The closets were easy because this is where most of the things you own but never use are stored. I sorted the items into sell, keep, donate, and throw away piles, always keeping in mind if there was still a use for the item.

For example, I have collected the soap and shampoo from hotels over the years. I never used them but figured I might be able to sell them. (I did later on at my sale. I packed them into zip-top plastic bags and sold them in bulk.)

Then I moved to the attic, basement, garage, and finally the individual rooms of my home. I went through every drawer and cupboard, looking for things I no longer needed or wanted and could sell for extra cash.

I priced things by looking up the going rate for each item on the Internet and made my stuff about one half of the current selling value. Everything I was selling was clean, organized into logical groups, and nothing was hard for buyers to see or reach. I printed signs from my computer for things like records and tapes and pasted them on the wall and the bins that held the items I'd grouped together. Everything that did not have a sign was individually priced. No one had to ask what the price was on an item, which made it so much easier to manage the sale.

To advertise my estate sale, I took pictures of the better items I had as well as broad-stroke pictures of the sale areas, and I posted them online, including in a Craigslist ad. I also took out a newspaper ad, with a link so people could see the photos.

I had eight friends help with the sale the first day to write up tickets, and then four came back to help the second day. All items were discounted the second day and at noon on the second day, I changed the sale to a bag sale.

TOSS	KEEP	SELL
Anything that's broken, cracked or has no second-life potential	Gifts and other decorative items that you use on a regular basis	Received gifts you're no longer interested in keeping but that might have resale value
Shoeboxes that are crushed or destroyed	Shoeboxes of all shapes and sizes—in good condition	I don't think shoeboxes have resale value but you could donate them to a local school
Crushed, torn, or soiled paper towel rolls	Paper towel rolls that you can put to good use immediately (no pack-ratting allowed)	Donate to a teacher who may be able to use them for future craft projects

At the end, virtually everything had sold with the exception of a few items of clothing and some furniture. Some of the things sold surprisingly well, such as old VHS tapes, CDs, and record albums, which sold for $2 each. I was also able to sell sewing projects that I'd started but never finished—I sold the fabric, patterns, and supplies for these. I also sold bags of pinecones and shells that I had collected over the years, rugs I no longer used and that I'd grown tired of, some vintage T-shirts from the '80s, and all of my Christmas, Halloween, and Easter decorations. I was even able to get rid of all of my holiday wrapping paper that I no longer wanted. As far as furniture went, I sold an old bedroom set, canopy bed, curio cabinet, chairs, the dining set, old travel trunks, an office desk, footstools, pillows, a love seat, and bookcases. Even the books and magazines sold.

By the end of the second day, I'd made $4,000 from the sale.

I'll be honest: In the two months leading up to my estate sale, my house was in a state of flux while I sorted and set the sale up. It was very stressful, but in the end the sale freed me from a lot of clutter, and it brought in enough money to pay off my car and a credit card bill.

I really don't think most people know how much stuff they have crammed into areas of their house that they don't see every day. My house was by no means a junk house. But every inch of storage space was full of things I'd collected and saved for someday, or projects I was going to finish but never did. Now when I open a closet, I feel free.

Total Cash Back in This Chapter

While we may not have made much money in this chapter from selling our stuff, Constance surely did. As you read in her "Cashing In" profile, she made a whopping $4,000 for her two-day estate sale. That anecdote aside, we've looked at some effective tips on how to save yourself from spending unnecessary cash, first by thinking about how to reduce what you already own and then how you can reuse items in new ways. In addition, I suggested that, rather than hire a pricey professional organizer or invest in expensive organizational tools that are pretty and color-coordinated, you could use items you already own—like old wedding gifts, shoeboxes, and paper-towel rolls—to get yourself organized.

Total Cash Back in This Chapter: **$4,384**

chapter 2

ORGANIZING THE LIVING AND FAMILY ROOMS

Families often spend much of their time together in a living room, family room, or den. If you and your family really *live* in your living room, it can get cluttered with stuff that belongs somewhere else or has no home anywhere else in the house—and your living room is just where it ends up. Common culprits are kids' backpacks, which they may have dropped there on their way in from school, or toys that never got put away and that belong in a toy box or your child's bedroom.

These are the rooms of a home where you should be able to spend time with your family—comfortably. And when I say comfortably I mean this: You shouldn't have to hopscotch across the floor to get from the room's entrance to the couch because there

Start Your Cleaning Engines

You can start straightening up in fifteen-minute bursts, with the "Toss, Keep, Sell" approach—meaning you'll think about each item you pick up in this way. Keep a trash bag or recycle bin with you for the things you determine you want to toss, and maybe have a box nearby into which you can place stuff you'd like to sell.

is a carpet of books, papers, video games, and other clutter on the floor.

In this chapter I'm going to help you organize your living room, family room, or den. I'm going to show you how you can turn clutter into beautiful decorations—trust me on this one—and help you to make sense of all of the media you might find in these rooms.

Creating a Clutter-Free Zone

Every home has a dumping ground—one place where the family drops the mail, kicks off their shoes, puts down their bags, and tosses anything else they're holding when they come in the door. In some homes there are multiple dumping grounds. This is often because the "normal" spot where the mail should go or the shoes should be stored is already overflowing so there's no space available, and then the family members move on to the next available horizontal surface and—wham!—they dump their stuff.

For a lot of families a favored dumping ground is the coffee table. It makes sense when you think about it: You come in from a long day and want to put your feet up. But first you'd like to look at the mail and maybe have a little snack from the groceries that you brought in from the car. Before you know it, your shoes are next to the coffee table, the mail is strewn across the top, and all the groceries that were stacked inside the shopping bags have spilled out on the coffee table or on the floor around it.

Now this use of the coffee table isn't a problem, unless after all of this dumping and spilling no one picks it up. So today's clutter ends up on top of yesterday's clutter and so on, and suddenly, you're balancing the mail on the arm of the couch or tossing it in the easy chair because there's no room left on the coffee table. Clearly, you need to change your cluttered ways, and I have some ideas on how you can do that.

MAKE IN-BOXES ON THE COFFEE TABLE

Flip through a home-furnishing catalog at some point and what do you see? Baskets, baskets, and more baskets. In my mind baskets can be a disheveled girl's best friend. They can be the tool you need to contain anything that you normally might have piled on the coffee table. When you place things in baskets, you leave the room looking a little less worse for the wear.

Ideally, you will get to a point where you will no longer need the crutch of baskets or can use fewer baskets as a way to temporarily clean up a room. But for now at least have baskets on hand so that if you need to neaten the room, you can do so quickly and in a somewhat organized fashion.

Here are some ways you can use these containers:

○ A basket for magazines, books, and other reading materials

○ A basket for loose change or orphaned pens

○ A basket for TV remotes, matches for the fireplace, or other items that belong in the living room

TIDY UP EVERY DAY

The key to keeping your living and family rooms neat is to tidy them up each night or morning—basically, once a day.

If your living room is currently a disaster, you may read this and say, "What? You're crazy. That will take too much time." Well, yes it certainly will, if you let the room get so out of control each day that you are looking at hours of work every time you try to make progress. But don't let that seemingly overwhelming task prevent you from doing anything at all.

If you get that room under control—where stuff isn't spilling off of every available surface—your daily straightening up will take only a few minutes. The notion here is maintenance and upkeep. And the more you do it, the less time you'll spend cleaning up.

When I stay on top of the straightening-up routine, I find that I can walk into a room and I feel like my *entire* life is under control—even if, in reality, it's only one room. Don't you want to feel that way, too?

DESIGNATE A SPOT FOR EVERYTHING IN THE LIVING ROOM

You've probably heard the old saying, "A place for everything and everything in its place." Well, in an organized home, that saying is the law.

If you don't already have designated spots for things in your home, make them and then communicate that with your family. Not only does this give you *bona fide* places to put things, but also when things get out of place, you know—and your family knows—exactly where to put them back.

Here are some ways we've put the "everything in its place" notion to work in our home:

○ **A mail bin.** My husband took a metal bin and put a big label on its side that read, "Mail only." We used to use this metal bin, filled with ice, to store drinks when we entertained. Now it's the place where the mail goes every day.

○ **A bench for shoes.** We have a bench with slide-out baskets underneath it, and this is where our kids know to put their shoes when they come in and take them off.

○ **A basket for remotes.** We have a small wicker basket that sits on top of our fireplace mantel, and it is the designated home for the TV remotes.

Thinning Your Reading Material

I have been in love with magazines since I was old enough to read. My parents first subscribed me to *Highlights* and *Ranger Rick*, and then I moved on to reading—and collecting—*Glamour*, *Teen*, and *Seventeen*. By the time I'd started sending my own stories to the magazines I loved to read, my room was overflowing with beloved back issues. I still remember my mother hiring someone to create a built-in bookcase for my room, most of which I filled with my magazines. What a shame she had to spend the money to do that when what I really should have been doing is thinning my magazine collection over time.

Fast forward a couple of decades, and I still have a love affair with the twenty magazines to which I subscribe. I know that I could easily cut my clutter by just reading my magazines online, but I enjoy the tactile experience of holding a magazine. Plus, when not writing books, I do write for magazines so I can justify subscribing to some of them.

Books can become just as problematic. I used to spend $800 a year on book purchases. But with more than twenty magazines coming in a month—some of them are weekly—I just had too much reading material in my house, even for someone who works in the industry. I don't have enough time in a day, week, or month to keep up with my magazines and books. Instead of being surrounded by useful tools for my trade, I find myself swimming through magazines and books I may never open. They usually end up in my living room—my favorite place to curl up with them.

If your living areas are also cluttered with reading material—no matter how worthy—try some of these tricks that I've started to institute to cut down while still feeding my love for the written word:

STOP SUBSCRIBING TO SOME MAGAZINES

For a long time I loved getting food magazines and trying recipes I found in those issues. But these days I'm more likely to get a cookbook or browse a blog than I am to tear a recipe out of a magazine. From time to time I might get a single issue of a food magazine but for the most part I've cut them from my magazine diet. Just cancelling the subscriptions for two magazines that I'd gotten for years saved me $27 and saved me from piles of clutter.

CULL MAGAZINES AFTER A CERTAIN TIME

Keep an eye on which magazines you actually read and when you read them. If you find yourself picking up the back-to-school issue of your favorite magazine between batches of holiday cookies in December or skimming through an article about skiing in July, it may be time to admit that those subscriptions aren't doing you much good. If an entire season has passed you by and you didn't read a magazine for that season, you never will. Make a deal with yourself that every other month (or whatever time frame works for you) you will cull your magazine collection.

FIND OTHER USES FOR YOUR MAGAZINES

So you can't part with your magazines just yet? Well, at least find other uses for them around the house so you can get them out of your living room.

Here are some reuses to consider:

O   Use them as makeshift hot pads in the kitchen.

O   Roll them up and stick them in your boots and shoes to help them maintain their shape. (This tip alone is a huge money saver; I saw "boot shapers" being sold for $50 a pair.)

O   Frame pretty pictures you find in magazines as decorations for your home.

LOCATE BOOKS YOU CAN SWAP OR SELL

Later on in the book, I dedicate chapters to making the most money possible from your stuff (Chapter 10) and learning how to swap what you own for other stuff (Chapter 11). In most instances with books and movies—the two things you're likely to have cluttering your living room, family room, or den—swapping is your best bet. These two items don't always bring in enough money to make it worth your while to sell them on eBay or at a garage sale, but they still have value.

Here's a brief introduction to the concept of swapping books and movies; you can turn to Chapter 11 for more in-depth information.

1. Look for hardcover and paperback books you've read and aren't interested in keeping or don't want to read again in the future.

2. Give your books' condition a thorough consideration. Books that have torn or missing pages, writing in them, or a musty smell don't do well for swapping. Plus, they have no place cluttering up your bookshelves. Get rid of them!

3. Start a book-swapping box or bag where you can store the books you identify as having swapping potential.

4. Find a book-swapping site you like so you can start trading your old books for new books you want to read.

These days I typically purchase a new book when I have a bookstore gift card or I need to buy a gift. Other than that I use book swapping or the good old library to supplement my reading. I may not be getting cold, hard cash for my old books, but I am saving myself hundreds.

 ## What's It Worth?

Maybe some of the clutter you're looking to get rid of in the living or family rooms is hanging on your walls. Well, before you toss those paintings out with the trash or sell them for a buck each at a garage sale, consider this: There is a chance that the painting that your grandmother handed down to you years ago may be worth something, albeit a *little* something.

"I think paintings can be one of the most impactful cash-for-clutter occurrences, because art is so subjective and can escalate in price very quickly," says Jeff Jeffers, CEO and principal auctioneer at Ohio-based Garth's Auctions Inc. (*www.garths.com*), a fifty-six-year-old national auction house that specializes in Americana, art, furniture, toys, firearms, jewelry, and a broad range of other antiques and historic items. Believe it or not, Jeffers says, there is a market for nearly any kind of art, whether it's a specific kind of painting or artist, a school of artists, or just a look that certain people like. "I might look at a painting on a wall and not personally like the aesthetic but there's a group that pays a lot of money for that style."

If you think that the paintings cluttering your walls might be worth something, Jeffers suggests you ask yourself these questions:

○ Is there a signature or any other kind of identifying information on the painting? Sometimes a signature is in the painting itself; other times it is on the back of the work, which you may or may not be able to see. Experts like Jeffers can use technology to check for a signature. If there isn't a signature, maybe there is a sticker on the back of the painting or a plaque on the front that may help you identify the artist. If not, you can try doing some Internet research based on the subject matter in the painting. "You may find a record or two of similar paintings," says Jeffers, and perhaps even the name of the artist.

○ How is the painting presented? Jeffers says that the average person may not realize that the quality of a frame often signifies the quality of what's *inside* the frame. And in some instances, frames themselves can be worth more than the painting they hold!

○ How long have I had this painting? If this painting has been in your family for years, that's a good thing. Because even if you're not sitting on an original Michelangelo, a fifty-year-old painting will fetch more money at auction than a five-year-old one. Jeffers likes to tell the story of a couple that came to him on one of his free appraisal days at his auction house. The couple had a pair of folk portraits, painted on wood, that they'd owned for twenty-five years. They mentioned that when they'd found the paintings in a storage locker they were cleaning out for a family member, someone had appraised them for $1,200 each years ago. Jeffers felt that they were probably worth a lot more and were likely pretty old—from the early nineteenth century. Eventually, the couple consigned the paintings for auction when Jeffers determined they were by a named artist. He thought they would fetch between $25,000 and $35,000, but the pair actually sold for $88,000.

○ What do I know about this painting's history? Jeffers says that the longer a painting stays in a family, the better it is for a painting's value because that helps you track the painting's ownership or *provenance—*

something art dealers want to know. Another of Jeffers's clients auctioned a painting that he had gotten from his grandfather and stored for decades in his basement. He was only the second owner of this painting, which Jeffers discovered was the work of a well-known Western artist. Because this man's grandfather had bought the painting new almost eighty years ago and had hung it in his own house for all those years, no one had ever seen this painting in public. It drew quite a lot of interest at auction and ended up selling for $180,000.

O   Is this actually a painting? To answer this question, you need to look closely at the painting's surface. Is there texture to the paint on the canvas (showing that it is likely an actual painting) or is the surface smooth and flat (meaning that it might be a well-executed print of a painting). That's not to say that a print doesn't have value—Jeffers says that certain prints do—but the value probably can't match that of an original oil by one of the masters.

Jeffers suggests that if you think you have something worth appraising—and don't know where you can take it—use the Internet to search for a local appraiser. For example, if you know the name of the artist on the painting is Smith, you could search "auction houses selling Smith." Even if the auction house you find is far away, there's no reason for you to incur shipping costs or drive halfway across the country for an appraisal. "Probably 30 percent to

40 percent of the time we are able to make a distinction about the quality and the authenticity of a work via photographs," he adds.

One last tip about selling something at auction: It should be a no-money-upfront proposition for the appraisal and auction. All monies will change hand after the auction is over, when the auctioneer gives you whatever he took in for your painting, minus his commission.

Using Clutter as Free Decorations

If you're a book lover like I am, you may need to do quite a bit of thinning of your collection from time to time. Thinning your reading collection occasionally is important, but what's really key is making your book collection work for you.

This usually involves organizing your bookshelves in one way or another. You can arrange books alphabetically by author, you can group by category, or you can do a combination of both—grouping by category, then alphabetizing within those categories. Doing so will help you identify any books you no longer want to keep and can get rid of to reduce your book clutter.

Now if you're a visual person like I am, you may be interested in a trick I recently learned: how to use books and other clutter as free decorations. You see, I tend to identify books by what the covers look like or by the color of the book's spine. For example, I still remember that the English-French and the English-Spanish dictionaries that I used in high school and college (and still own) both happen to be red.

With this vibrant idea in mind, I decided to organize my books by color. This helped me not only to get my books in order in a way that makes sense for me—and possibly you, too—but also I ended up with neat and tidy shelves that are actually quite pretty. Pictures from my bookshelf transformation are in Chapter 11.

Here's how I accomplished that task:

1. I remembered the ROYGBIV mnemonic from my school days so I could arrange my books, by shelf, in color order. (That's red, orange, yellow, green, blue, indigo, violet.)

2. Then, color by color, I grabbed books from the living room and around the house that fit these color categories.

3. In my search I decided to modify the color categories to be more like ROYGBVWB—combining indigo and violet, and adding white and black to the mix.

4. I identified the two standing bookcases where I wanted to place my books by color, then I emptied those shelves.

5. After a good dusting I started loading up the books by color. I didn't spend too much time doing a secondary organizing by book size, because I wanted to get this task done quickly. Plus, I knew that a lack of uniformity in how I stacked or stood up the books would offer a better-looking end result.

6. Once all the books were grouped by color on the shelves, I added in a few housewares in similar colors just to give it a finishing touch. This ranged from a small purple vase (for the violet shelf) to a decorative green plate (for the green shelf) to a framed turquoise butterfly (for the blue shelf).

Cashing In
Michele, Maryland

My clutter came about because I was basically combining the stuff from three houses into one—mine and my husband's, my stepdad's (and my late mom's), and stuff from both of my grandmothers' that my mom had kept in her house. While going through the stuff, I could immediately tell that some would have to be donated. This comes from my own experience of visiting antique shops, yard sales, and flea markets over the years. With many of the pieces we just weren't sure. We had a feeling we could get money for some of the items, but we weren't sure how much. We brought in appraisers to tell us what some of the things were worth.

Once my husband and I found out what we could expect to get for different pieces of furniture, we decided to try selling them on our own rather than go through an auction. We chose the most attractive pieces that we thought would sell—two pieces of art deco furniture, a piece with intricate carving, and a desk.

I decided to sell the pieces through Facebook. I just posted straight up that it was my grandmother's art deco furniture. There was nothing fancy in terms of the writing—I just posted the measurements and *a lot of photos, especially those that could show the art deco attributes. Word got around and we ended up selling a dresser and dry sink to a Facebook friend in New Jersey, who paid $400 for the pieces.*

It was interesting to realize that often times there are people who really want something that you may think is utter crap. We had an ugly metal rooster that we'd inherited. We posted it on Facebook and had so many people clamoring for it, it was nuts! It went to a friend in South Carolina who loves the USC team whose mascot is a rooster, Mr. Cocky.

I also had a Snoopy bank that I thought was ugly, and it had been sitting in a box in my basement for years. We ended up making $300 on it.

The point is that there are folks who collect everything. If you're not sure about an item, look on eBay or go to someone who knows. You may just have a gem sitting in your basement.

Decluttering Your Decorations

While your collection of magazines and books won't add a lot to your savings account, the tchotchkes and other bric-a-brac that you use to decorate your living room, family room, and den might.

In Chapter 1, I talked about how one of the biggest contributors to a clutter problem can be all the wedding, birthday, and anniversary gifts you may have received over the years—and held onto because you feel guilty about getting rid of them. You may have some of those gifts somewhere on display or stuffed into a wall unit or cabinets in your living room or family room. There's no reason for you to hold onto them if they don't bring you pleasure and if you're not using them. Plus, they could be bringing in some much needed cash while cleaning off your shelves and clearing out your clutter.

DECORATIONS THAT BRING IN DOLLARS

In a recent survey on my Suddenly Frugal blog, many people reported taking in decent amounts of cash for bric-a-brac and household decorations they no longer wanted. One survey taker wrote, "I made over $200 at a flea market from selling a bunch of tchotchkes. People love home-decor items." Think about what you are currently using to decorate the walls or shelves of your living room, family room, or den. If there are any things you don't absolutely love, now is a great time to consider selling those items.

ELECTRONICS YOU NO LONGER NEED

Referencing my Suddenly Frugal survey again, people reported making money from stereo and TV electronics, all of which you may have stored in these rooms of your home. For example, when my kids were little, we invested in two VCRs. We used one upstairs and one downstairs so that the kids could watch their favorite movies in multiple places. Eventually we moved on to DVD players, and then TiVo and cable on demand. These days those VCRs and DVD players are collecting dust in the TV cabinet in the living room. Some of the to-sell items on my to-do list include the VCRs and DVD player. Even if I take in $25 or $50 for them, that's better than having them sitting around, getting dusty. (I'll also check out their value on *www.gazelle.com*, a website that buys used electronics for cash and which I explain in greater detail in Chapter 9.)

Quick Clutter Challenge

While you may still enjoy the whir of a VHS tape in the VCR, technology has made it much easier to declutter our living spaces. On-demand cable and DVR programs give us plenty of freedom to clear shelves of outdated and bulky technology, so challenge yourself to turn obsolete clutter into cash!

Set your timer for fifteen minutes and see what kind of unused electronics you can uncover. Are there VCRs and DVD players underneath your stereo receiver and TiVo? Do you have portable DVD players your kids used before you got an in-car DVD system, but which you haven't used lately? While you won't recoup your initial investment, I feel confident that you could sell these items and easily get at least $100 for them.

Set your timer and ready, set, go!

VIDEO GAMES THAT HAVE FALLEN OUT OF FAVOR

Have you upgraded your video-gaming system lately? If so, then what are you doing with all of those old video games that you can no longer play in your new system? Did you know that there's a market for them—beyond the crazy prices for vintage video games? Some stores will buy back your old video games and give you a store credit so you can buy new video games. They'll also buy old gaming systems and give you a discount when purchasing a new gaming system. Though you're not walking out with cash in your pocket, if you're a gaming family, this is an excellent way to get the video games you want without spending more money acquiring games. Also, with the incentive to trade in old games for store credit, you can get into a regular routine of thinning your video game collection—thus cutting down on your clutter—and knowing that when you want a new game down the road, you'll have a credit toward that purchase, if not be able to buy it outright. (Swapping sites that deal in DVDs also deal in video games. Turn to Chapter 11 for more about that.)

Selling a Piano

Where I grew up most of my friends' houses had a piano in their living room or family room. So did my house, my husband's childhood home, and the house we currently live in. We were very lucky to inherit a piano; I feel like a house isn't a home without one.

Years ago our daughters took piano lessons, as I did when I was their age, and every once in a while I would sit down at the piano and tickle the old ivories. To say that our piano is used on a regular basis, however, would be a gross overstatement. I think the last time someone lifted the cover over the keys and sat down and played was two Decembers ago, when my mother was visiting and feeling nostalgic for some Christmas carols (she grew up playing piano, too). Because the piano has become just another piece of furniture in our living room—dare I say clutter in our living room—I would probably be justified in wanting to sell it. But our piano was my husband's grandmother's piano, and when it comes to that instrument, sentiment will win out over function every time.

That's not to say that every family feels as strongly about a piano, and maybe it's time for you to sell yours. If so, you'll be happy to hear that pianos tend to hold a decent amount of value over time. It's not unheard of for a twenty-year-old upright piano (versus a grand piano) to sell for between $400 and $800. That's especially true if you have a brand-name piano, such as Steinway, Yamaha, or Baldwin.

If it's been a while since you've had your piano tuned and you're thinking of selling it, you may want to invest the time and money to bring in someone to do that. It will cost around $75 or $100 to have the piano tuned, but it could mean the difference between getting $400 and $800 for your piano. If a music lover with a good ear comes to buy your piano and hears that it's out of tune, that person may offer you a low-ball price. This person knows that he or she is going to have to hire a tuner on the other end, so why pay top dollar for your piano when there will be out-of-pocket costs for tuning in the near future?

Of course, if the piano you're looking to offload is a family heirloom, was built in the early part of the twentieth century, or has other "magical" qualities that you believe make it worthy of something better than Craigslist, have it looked at by an auction-eer that specializes in musical instruments. If you have no idea where to find such an expert, visit the *Antiques Roadshow* website on *www.pbs.org*, and then search under "appraisers" by specialty. A handful come up under the "musical instruments" category, and if you click on their names, you'll find contact information for them at their places of business, which include Christie's in New York City and Skinner in Boston.

Be careful that you don't end up working with an appraiser that also restores pianos: I've heard of situations where these so-called appraisers were really there to talk customers into thousands of dollars of restorations costs, with the promise of a big auction pay-day after the piece had been restored. In many instances, the piano

TOSS	KEEP	SELL
Items that are cracked and broken, or have no resale value	Decorative pieces and house-wares you got as gifts that you love and use	Anything from a well-known manufacturer or store (like Tiffany) that someone will want to buy
Magazines older than six months	Magazines that are less than six months old	Vintage copies of popular magazines
Recycle broken/non-working electronics	Electronics you're currently using	Electronics that still have a market value
Cracked or scratched video games	Video games you currently use	Used video games, especially if they have a "vintage" quality

owner ends up paying tons of money upfront for these restorations, only to have none of those auction promises come true. Of course, that's not to say that all appraisers and piano restorers work this way, but beware that there are some who do not have you and your piano's best interests in mind.

Total Cash Back in This Chapter

It's amazing how much income potential you can uncover once you start looking for it. You may have had no idea that a wedding gift you'd held onto for so many years was worth reselling or that a painting you'd picked up at yard-sale prices would actually have enough value to sell at auction. At the very least you may uncover old electronics and other decorative items that may be obsolete in your mind but very valuable to someone else.

Total
Cash Back in
This Chapter:
$1,577

chapter 3

DECLUTTERING YOUR DINING ROOM

Dining rooms by their very nature are magnets for clutter. That's because most of the furniture you have in the typical dining room—china cabinet, curio, and buffet/serving table—is designed to store things. With this intended function, it's almost as if you have implied permission to stuff them to the gills with your china, silver, crystal, and table linens, and whatever else it is you store in the dining room. I know that there have been times when I've tried to smoosh so much into my breakfront that I couldn't close the drawers or shut the cabinet doors. That should have been my first clue that I had a dining room clutter problem, but alas I kept on as usual, acquiring more stuff for that room and then trying to find somewhere in the dining room to store it.

Now, I'm all about streamlining what I keep in the dining room. I decide what stays by taking stock of what I actually use when I entertain, not what I might possibly need one day—say when the Queen of England shows up on my doorstep for tea.

In this chapter I'm going to help you also to streamline what you store in your dining room and to figure out how to keep that room clutter free. This way the next time the Queen *does* stop by—or maybe you just want to finally host Thanksgiving dinner for your family—you'll have a neat, tidy, and clean space where you can serve those special people in your life.

Determine What's in Your Dining Room

Let's get ready to have a soul-cleansing and china cabinet–clearing experience. We're going to throw open all the curio doors and pull out all the sideboard drawers, and take a good, hard look at what you're storing in the dining room. If you've got stuff piled deep inside these pieces of furniture, make time and room to take everything out. You can lay it out on your dining room table (unless it's covered in stuff) or put it on the floor. I'm guessing that you are going to find tons of things that seem logical to keep in the dining room but, in reality, should have been stashed somewhere else long ago—if not gotten rid of altogether.

TAKING INVENTORY

Start by looking for the following items that you may have stored in the dining room and that you can put aside for recycling or throwing in the trash:

○ Stained or torn linens

○ Chipped, cracked, or stained dishes, vases, and other serving pieces

○ Sets of candlesticks, napkin rings, or other pairs that are mismatched or missing pieces

Make sure that you have a bag or bin nearby so that you can throw away anything that is clearly trash, including old wrappers, bubble wrap from a long-ago move, paper, boxes, and more. We're talking about the stuff that stuff comes *in*. None of this should have been left behind when you unpacked weeks, months, or years ago when you moved into your home. Or, maybe you left your "one day this will serve a purpose" purchases in their shopping bags and boxes in the dining room because you had no idea where to actually store this new stuff.

Next, take a good look at the items that are left. Does everything that you're going through belong in the dining room, or did it get stashed there during a dump-and-run moment? For example, when I was in the process of streamlining what I kept in my china cabinet, I found Christmas linens mixed in with the everyday stuff. My red-and-green placemats, table runners with snowflakes on them, and silver angel napkin rings all should have been stored away in the Christmas decoration boxes that I keep in my attic (see Chapter 7, Decluttering Your Laundry Room, Garage, Basement, and Attic) until the holidays roll around again.

Sure, it might seem logical to keep *all* the linens in one place, regardless of the time of year it is. But what we're trying to accomplish here is clearing out the clutter. Your mission is to get rid of anything you've been storing that either you don't really need anymore or that should really be stored long term somewhere other than the dining room.

Finally, be honest about how many tablecloths, cloth napkins, napkins rings, and whatever else you keep in the dining room you actually need. For starters, what are the chances that you've held onto tablecloths that someone in your family handed down to you but which don't actually fit any tables you own? Yes, you may *one day* own an oval table that your grandmother's tablecloth would look lovely on, but until that day, why is it taking up space in your dining room? Either put that tablecloth in a hope chest—because you can't bear to part with it—hand it down to a relative who *can* use it, or put it in your "to sell" pile. This will allow you to clear out the space it was taking up and, ideally, get you some cash for your clutter.

As far as how many types and number of pieces of table linens you should keep stored in your dining room, here are some ball-park figures to work with:

O Eight to twelve cloth napkins—or however many place settings of dishes you have when you use your dining room

O Eight to twelve placemats or, again a number that works with how many place settings of dishes you have

O Two tablecloths—one light, one dark

O Two table runners

What should you do with everything left over? Sell them to bring in extra cash!

ORGANIZING SERVING PIECES

Though I've had problems with a cluttered dining room in the past, I believe I can never have enough serving pieces. Even for our nightly dinner together as a family, I put all the food out on serving pieces. I can justify keeping these pieces—about eight of them—in my china cabinet, even post-decluttering, because I genuinely love them and use them regularly. It wasn't always this way with my serving pieces, however.

I mentioned earlier in this book about the guilt I used to feel about dinnerware I'd received as gifts and felt I had to use—especially when the gift giver came to dinner—and this was true for serving pieces I *used to have*. I emphasize that because, when decluttering any part of your house, it's important only to keep on hand the items you know, love, and use on a regular basis. Everything else? Well, it belongs in the "toss" or "sell" pile.

As you get ready to organize your serving pieces, think about the things that you are holding onto because you feel you should or because you feel guilty about getting rid of them. Anything that falls into that keep-by-guilt category should leave your home—and in this case your dining room—immediately.

So do you have a sterling-silver serving set (fork, spoon, ladle) that requires polishing, was a wedding present, and now it's all tarnished and you've never touched it? Well, since you've never used it and can't imagine you ever will, put it aside to sell.

What about the platter that your cousin got you during a Polly-anna gift exchange last Christmas? If it's not your taste, don't keep it around.

See where I'm going with this?

In order to achieve a truly clutter-free dining room, you need to have on hand only the useful things that don't come with guilt attached.

PUTTING EVERYTHING BACK

As you start to put everything back that you'd taken out during this inventory period, think logically about how you store what you've decided to keep. For example, maybe in the past you put the napkin rings in with other dining room knick-knacks, and then folded up the cloth napkins and stashed them with the placemats. This time around store items that work in concert together. So the napkin rings and cloth napkins should go in the same drawer and, if the drawer is big enough, the placemats, too. In another drawer keep the tablecloths and the table runners together, since when you're setting out a table, you will likely use these together.

If you don't have enough drawers in your current dining room for storage, then you're going to have to come up with an alternate storage plan. Can you hang your tablecloths in an unused closet? Would an open shelving/storage system work for you?

One of the reasons I like open shelving is that your linens and other supplies can double as decorations. So find a large bowl that you might normally keep tucked away somewhere, and put it out, front and center, with your napkin rings collected in it. Then roll up all of your cloth napkins as tightly as possible and stick them in a vase like a bunch of blossom-less flowers. This will allow you to creatively store what you've decided to keep in your dining room. And if you are committed to keeping everything out in the open, you may have an easier time keeping the space clutter free, because you will see everything every time you walk into the room.

Cashing In
Alicia, New York

One day my adult son told me that he'd been selling stuff on eBay and suggested I give it a try. He told me, "Mom, people will buy anything."

It wasn't easy at first to go through our stuff and decide what to sell. I kept asking myself, "Do we really need this?" I made three piles: keep, homeless shelter/Goodwill, and sell.

When I had difficulty deciding which pile to put things in, I would remember what my sister-in-law had told me when she was clearing out her own clutter. "Have no mercy!" I would chant this in difficult times, and then put the item in the pile to sell or to donate. I never ended up keeping anything I had hesitated over. My main goal was to declutter, not to make money, but when it was time to start pricing things and figure out where I was going to sell them, I did research on Amazon, eBay, and Craigslist. Then I took good pictures and wrote great descriptions, and started listing stuff.

I ended up selling four ways.

I sold books and CDs on both Amazon and eBay. I got anywhere from $2 to $20 for them.

For designer clothing, jewelry, makeup, and other things I could easily ship, I stuck with eBay. I sold Brooks Brothers suits for $60 to $75 each, and shirts for $15 to $20 each. Makeup went for $2 to $25, and one perfume I had, that I know came from Bergdorf Goodman, sold for $150. I even sold sheets, tablecloths, and shower curtains!

For things that I couldn't ship or wrap, I used Craigslist. I sold a pair of antique chairs that way and got $600.

Eventually, I found this bulletin board in a local professional complex with lots of doctors' offices in it, and I offloaded a lot of my kids' stuff that way, such as strollers and baby swings. I made about $200 for all of them.

Dos and Don'ts for Keeping Your Dining Room Table Clear

What is it about the open, horizontal space of a dining room table that makes it such a tempting spot on which to pile things? Is it because most of us don't use our formal dining rooms on a daily basis, therefore we can hide our messes in there? Is it because dining room tables by their very nature are oversized, so when we need a space to spread out a project, it calls out to us? I know that people who homeschool their kids or work from home—and don't have a dedicated classroom space or office—often end up working at the dining room table. While this is fine for the time being, the key is to clean up after yourself. My guess is that because of the hidden nature of most dining rooms, we don't end up putting stuff away at the end of our lessons or conference calls, and soon enough the dining room table is piled high with papers.

With that in mind, here are some dos and don'ts for keeping your dining room table clear of non–dining room clutter:

○ Do figure out why you are working at the dining room table versus somewhere else in the house. Is it because you have no place to fold your laundry (see Chapter 7) or your home office has become a de facto storage locker (see Chapter 9: Getting Your Home Office under Control)?

○ Don't put more than one project at a time on top of the dining room table.

○ Do keep a basket, box, or container nearby that you can put your stuff into whenever you are finished working on something at the dining room table.

○ Do clean off the table into the aforementioned baskets, boxes, or containers at the end of the day. Otherwise tomorrow's pile will grow on top of today's pile, and before you know it, a paper monster will having taken over your dining room table.

○ Don't keep the leaves in your dining room table when you're not using it. Making the table smaller will make it a less inviting place to spread your work out.

○ Do keep the dining room table covered with a tablecloth if you'd like to try to break your habit of using it as your workspace. I find it difficult to write on a surface covered in fabric and maybe you will, too. This may force you to finally clear out your home office or whatever space you've been avoiding using because it's too messy to be functional.

○ Do keep the dining room table set for a "future" dinner party (even if you have none planned). You'll be less likely to disturb your beautifully set table by plopping clutter on top of it.

What's It Worth?

Like most brides I chose a china pattern when I got married. And though my husband and I liked the design we chose, I never got around to adding more pieces to our set. In fact, since tying the knot in 1992, I never even got around to *using* the china, except for Thanksgiving the first year we were married. After that the only time we ever took out the china was when we were packing up to move houses and needed to wrap it in bubble wrap once again. We've been in our current house for three years, and guess what? We haven't even bothered to unpack it into our china cabinet. What does it matter that the pattern is memorable and beautiful or that the set wasn't too expensive to add to if it's gone unused and untouched for years?

A few years ago I thought about selling the pieces on eBay, but my husband suddenly became sentimental over this china. He thought we should *buy* additional pieces on eBay so we would have twelve place settings, and then we could finally use it for formal occasions. But the truth is we're not very formal people. We love our everyday, colorful, dishwasher-safe dishes that we always use when we entertain. The china, on the other hand, must be hand washed and is so impractical.

Since we never did get around to buying additional place settings, I've started secretly looking into selling the china again. It's doing us no good sitting in the basement when it could be bringing in some cash and freeing up a couple of basement shelves.

I found a great potential way to sell the china that doesn't involve eBay or an auctioneer. I've been in touch with a North Carolina business called Replacements (*www.replacements.com*). This company has made a name for itself by tracking down difficult-to-locate pieces of china, silver, and other serving pieces, and

Quick Clutter Challenge

Old cloth napkins can turn a beautiful table setting into an embarrassment, but when they have finally taken too much wear and tear, they make great dusting tools and cleaning rags. Wouldn't it be nice to save money on paper towels by reusing something you were going to throw out anyway?

For this Quick Clutter Challenge, find the cloth napkins you would never put out for company, the ones in a stained, torn, or worn-out state, and gather them up to store with your cleaning supplies. Are you ready to set your timer for fifteen minutes? Ready, set, go find some cloth napkins that are past their prime and that you can transform into reusable "paper" towels.

selling it to people who have discontinued china patterns or hard-to-find pieces. I know folks who have used Replacements after finding and buying just a few place settings at an antique store. Replacements was able to fill in the holes in the set—from extra place settings to serving dishes.

Turns out that one of the ways that Replacements gets its stock of 300,000 china patterns is by buying china from people like me who no longer want it. (Replacements also buys old china at auctions and antique stores.) The process for selling your china to Replacements is pretty straightforward. You call the company (800-737-5223), tell them what kind of china you are offering, and the person on the phone can tell you right away whether or not Replacements is currently buying stock of the china you want to sell. I found out that Replacements *is* in the market for pieces from my pattern, and after taking down my contact information, they e-mailed me an offer.

If I packed up my china and sent it to Replacements within thirty days of their e-mailed offer, here's what I could get for my china (note: This is just a sampling of their offer since the list they sent was about thirty items long):

O $6 cup-and-saucer set

O $7 dinner plate

O $7 luncheon plate/accent plate

O $5 salad plate

O $2 bread-and-butter plate

- ○ $5 all-purpose bowl

- ○ $23 larger soup bowl

- ○ $70 round vegetable serving dish with cover

- ○ $12 small oval serving platter

- ○ $22 larger oval serving platter

- ○ $24 gravy boat and under plate

- ○ $24 teapot with lid

Because I didn't receive or purchase serving pieces, I couldn't take advantage of the whopping $70 they were offering for a round, covered, vegetable-serving dish. However, I do have eight place settings that include the cup and saucer set (total: $48), dinner plate (total: $56), luncheon plate (total: $56), salad plate (total: $40), and all-purpose bowl (total: $40).

Replacements qualified its offer with this statement: "We cannot buy pieces with chips, cracks, stains, or excessive wear." Considering how little my china has been used since I originally received it, I feel confident that I could easily get $240 for stuff I have just sitting in a box in the basement. Of course, it hurts to know that my family spent about $100 *per place setting* when they bought the china new, but it's better to get $240 in my pocket now rather than to worry about what someone once paid for china that I'm never going to use anyway.

TOSS	KEEP	SELL
Broken, cracked, or chipped china and other serving pieces	China or place settings of dishes that you use on a regular basis	Any china or serving pieces you've either never touched or haven't used recently—and can't imagine you'll use again in the near future
Stained, ripped, or soiled table linens (turn what you can into rags, if possible)	Eight to twelve cloth napkins and placemats, and one or two table cloths and table runners each	Overruns of any table linens you no longer want
Uneven numbers of or mismatched serving pieces, such as napkin rings, candlestick holders, and flatware	Just enough serving pieces to match the number of place settings you own	Extra serving pieces and table accessories that are in good condition and which you can't envision yourself using in the future

Freeing Up Floor Space

As you near the end of your dining room decluttering, you may discover that you no longer need all the dining room pieces in that space anymore. Chances are that along the way you acquired the china cabinet, curio, and hutch because you had so much dining room stuff you needed to store. At this point you should have thinned your collection—even if it's just from a linens standpoint—and maybe you can give up a piece of furniture as well. You can move it to another room where you can put it to better use, or maybe this is an opportunity to sell that piece of furniture and put some cash in your pocket.

Once my husband and I accepted the fact that we were never going to put our good china back in the china cabinet, let alone use it when we have company over for dinner, we found that we didn't actually need a china cabinet. We ended up giving it to friends who were moving into a new house, and didn't have the money for any dining room furniture. Otherwise, I would have sold it on Craigslist.

Without the china cabinet, we were left with a single hutch and a fold-down buffet table (which can double as a second dining room table if we're entertaining a big crowd), and that was all we needed to make our dining room a functional, clutter-free space.

Total Cash Back in This Chapter

When it comes to your dining room, I believe there's more to be gained by decluttering this room so you can enjoy a neater, more organized environment than there is from the money you might make from selling your stuff. When you have people over for special occasions, the dining room is where you are most likely to do your entertaining. You deserve to have a neat and orderly space where you can serve your guests a meal and enjoy their company. That said, if you registered for china for your wedding but never got around to using it, at least you know there's a resource you can go to and get some cash back for those dishes and serving pieces.

Total Cash Back in This Chapter: **$240**

chapter 4

BETTERING YOUR BATHROOM ORGANIZATION

In my house, a big part of the preparation for the daily dash out the door occurs in the bathroom. My husband rushes to shave—and leaves his razor out on the counter because there was no place to put it. My kids shower in the morning—and leave their towels bunched up on the floor either because there was no more room on a towel rack or because no one had emptied the overflowing laundry hamper. For a while, the lack of organization in our bathroom was making our mornings chaotic, and the mess that people were leaving behind showed it. However, once we took the time to streamline what we stored in the bathroom and how we organized our toiletries and other essentials, we had a calmer time during the morning rush—which wasn't much of a rush at all anymore—and fewer messes to clean up in the long run.

Evaluate Each of Your Bathrooms

You can't begin to calm the chaos in your bathroom until you can identify where the craziness is centered. That said, let's start by evaluating how you use your bathrooms and what you store in them.

If your home has more than one bathroom, each one will likely require a different kind of organizing based on how your family uses it. Whenever possible, I'll separate out advice for the three types of bathrooms that most multi-bathroom homes have: master bathrooms, guest/hallway/kids' bathrooms, and powder rooms.

DAILY USE OF YOUR BATHROOMS

Take a walk around your house and go stand in the doorway of one of your bathrooms. Now think about what exactly occurs in this bathroom on a daily basis. Is it like our master bathroom, chaos central for the daily rush to leave the house? Is it the bathroom where your kids perform their periodic extreme makeovers? Or is it a place that only guests use on occasion?

Now look at the bathroom with a fresh set of eyes. What do you see? Are your countertops cluttered with remnants of the daily routine? Are there hair styling lotions, potions, and tools scattered about? Where are the towels that people use after bathing or washing their hands? How is your supply of toilet paper, toothpaste, and more? Are there things in the bathroom that belong in another room?

Asking yourself these questions and giving each bathroom a once-over will give you an honest evaluation of how your bathrooms are used on a daily basis and what evidence is left behind.

Take Out the Trash

Don't spend any money on expensive trash bags to line tiny bathroom trash bins. Use a plastic shopping bag in these trash cans instead. Better yet, before you line the trash bins with a bag, stuff a couple of those plastic bags in the bottom. That way whenever you empty the trash, you won't have to put off finishing the task because you can't find a replacement liner: It will be right there in the bin.

This exercise isn't to change how the members of your family do what they need to do in the bathroom each day or to point fingers at those family members who don't clean up after themselves. Rather, this process should help you start thinking about how you can help make the daily routine easier on everyone—and the cleanup from it even simpler.

Clear Countertop Clutter

When you go into one of your bathrooms, what do you see on the countertop? In an organized bathroom, you should see very little on the countertops—maybe soap for washing hands after using the toilet, and toothbrushes and toothpaste—not everything scattered all over the place. It's even fine if you'd like to keep a small musical device in a bathroom with a shower, so you can be entertained

Photo © DIGISTOCK

Wouldn't you like to start each morning with a countertop that looks like this?

while washing up. But other than that, there shouldn't be anything else left on top of the counter. Everything in your bathroom should have a home so that cleanup is a snap, because you know where everything belongs.

In the master bathroom and the hallways/kids' bathroom that my children use, there are many items that we use on a daily basis to either get ready for school/work or at the end of the day to clean up before bed. There is no reason for any of those items to be left lying around. That's why we've adopted some of these storage methods for items that were formerly known as countertop clutter.

We're using:

O Small pegboards that my husband mounted on a wall near the countertop. We use these to hang up the flat iron, curling iron, blow dryer, and electric shaver charger after people have finished using them. (A simple slipknot in the cord helps to hang these up.)

O Makeup bags, dopp kits, and bins to hold each person's daily necessities. My husband's dopp kit contains his daily medication, shaving cream, and razor. For my daughters and me, our makeup kits have our makeup (naturally), any hair products and accessories we use, and daily medication and vitamins.

O Oversized coffee mug or small plant vase in which we stand up our toothbrushes and toothpaste tubes.

O Large basket to hold daily miscellany. I use this basket to store items that each family member likely uses on a daily basis but for which no one person could claim ownership. Therefore it wouldn't make sense to put these things in a person's dopp kit or makeup bag, and it surely doesn't make sense to spend extra money on duplicates just so someone could call it his or her own. Some of this daily miscellany includes cotton swabs, makeup remover, and floss.

Stop Just Stashing Towels

How many people use each bathroom on a daily basis? And do you actually have enough towel racks to accommodate each person that uses that bathroom? You should have, at minimum, one towel rack per person per bathroom for the big bath towels that they use when drying off after a shower. If you have girls like I do, who like to use a separate towel for wrapping up their hair after washing it, then you should increase your towel rack minimum to two racks per person per bathroom—or one very large towel rack per person per bathroom. Clearly, in a powder room that is only used occasionally you don't need these large racks. But to make sure there's always a hand towel available at any of your sinks, you will need one towel rack per sink in each bathroom.

Using this formula you can tell right away if you don't have enough towel racks for the ways that people in your house use towels. And if you don't have enough space for hanging them up, this could be the solution to the towel clutter problem in your bathroom. If your family simply does not have any place to hang up their towels, how can you blame them for dropping them on the floor or laying them across the counter?

While you can get away with pegboards for hanging up most things in your home, I would recommend that when it comes to towels, you splurge on actual towel racks. If you don't spread out your towels to dry each time you use them, they will take more time to dry out and will end up smelling like mildew faster—meaning more laundry for you to do in the long run.

Can't figure out where you could possibly put more towel racks? Here are some spots to consider:

○ Behind the bathroom door

○ On the shower wall

○ Double hung on the wall

○ Under the window

Now that you know where to *hang up* your towels, what about where you *store* extra towels? Do you have a designated spot for these? Currently, I do not have access to a traditional linen closet, so my husband installed a set of wire shelves above the toilets in each of the bathrooms with showers. Then I take clean towels and roll them up, and stack them like loaves of bread. This open-air storage system helps keep our bathroom orderly in two ways:

1. Everyone in the family knows where to go when he or she needs a new towel.

2. With a quick glance at those shelves, I can tell if it's time to throw a load of towels into the laundry.

How Many Towels?

The linen closet door won't close and the hamper is always stuffed with once-used towels. Is part of your bathroom clutter problem the fact that you have *too many* bath towels? If you are struggling to find shelf space or to handle bulky loads of bathroom laundry at once, think about thinning your towel collection.

Two bath towels per person, per bathroom is sufficient. If a person's only two towels are dirty, that person has no choice but to wash, dry, and put them away—keeping your laundry clutter in check, too! If the rest of your towels are in ratty shape, you can turn them into rags, or donate them to an animal shelter. If the leftover towels are still presentable, put them aside in longer-term storage for when overnight guests come to visit, or try to sell them when you have your next yard sale.

In the powder rooms, I keep a basket of rolled hand towels, similar to the bread-loaf look I referenced above. This basket sits on the floor, in a corner of the powder room. Again, it's functional in that people always know where to look when they need a new towel to dry their hands, and I can see when I need to restock the hand towels with a quick glance at that basket. Also, having this basket of rolled towels doubles as a quasi-decoration for the powder room.

If you don't currently have a permanent home for your towels, you should make one. Could you put towels folded in a closet or under the sink? Or what about rolling them up like I do and stashing them in a basket or on open-air shelves? If all else fails you could always store each person's towels in his or her bedroom and solve the towel problem altogether.

Rethink Under-Sink Storage

Unless your bathrooms all have pedestal sinks in them, you may have a ton of under-sink storage in the bathroom vanity that you could be taking advantage of as you work toward getting your bathroom organized. Or maybe that area inside the vanity is at the heart of your clutter problem. I know that in addition to my countertop clutter issues, I also had a problem with just tossing things underneath the sink. So did everyone else in my family.

This area inside the vanity was where I threw things when I needed to clean up in a hurry—"Oh, no, company showed up unexpectedly and my bathroom is a sty!"—or when I simply did not know where to put something that I thought belonged in the bathroom. So under the sink it went, for an out-of-sight, out-of-mind approach to cleaning up. But as I write about later on in Chapter 7, Decluttering the Laundry Room, Garage, Basement, and Attic, it is this kind of short-term approach that gets you in long-term trouble with clutter. Here's why.

When you store things haphazardly, you lose track of what you've stored and where you've stored it. Then when you need

Extend the Life of Your Medicine

If you're supposed to take a daily pill, it makes sense to keep it in the bathroom where you can take it as soon as you get up. But many prescription medicine labels warn you *not* to keep them in a moist environment, such as your bathroom, as moisture can break down the medication's potency. As you organize, find a bowl, box, or basket that you can put all of your medications into, and then relocate it to another part of the house where you won't risk damaging the medicine. A good place might be in your kitchen, where you're likely to go each morning anyway. Plus, you'll have cut down your medication clutter!

Note: If you have small children in the house, always store medicines in a safe, secure spot where curious minds and prying fingers cannot find them.

that thing or something like it, you have no idea where to look for it. So you waste time searching around your house, and you're likely to end up at the store, buying a new copy or version of the thing you need. And wouldn't you know it? Soon thereafter you find the original item you had. Now you've got two of them to store, and you've spent money that you wouldn't have had to spend had you known where the item was in the first place. Hopefully, you won't make the storage mistake again and, some time in the near future, end up with *three* identical things. (I speak from experience here.)

This is as true for the under-sink storage in your bathrooms as it is for *any room* of your house. If your approach to straightening up your bathroom is a dump-and-run, you could also be stashing things that your family may need on a daily basis—like shampoo, conditioner, soap, toilet paper, and toothpaste—in places they can't find them.

Here are some steps to help you stop this dump-and-run madness underneath your bathroom sink:

1. Clear out everything from under the bathroom sink or in your vanities.

2. Throw away anything that is clearly garbage, such as the plastic wrapping from a new package of cosmetics that someone may have tossed under the sink instead of in the trash can in the first place. (My kids are guilty of this from time to time.)

3. Use your favorite cleaning product and a rag to wipe down inside the vanity. No reason to clean out the space and not clean out the *schmutz*.

4. Of the stuff you've pulled out from under the vanity, begin grouping like things together.

5. Once you have everything divided by category, take a look at what you've got. See if there are things buried in those piles that really belong in the circular file, i.e. the trash. For example, in the medical pile, what are the expiration dates on some of the medicines and antibiotic creams you've found? If you are within a couple of months of when those items expired, you're

probably okay. But if you find tubes or tablets with expiration dates from years ago, throw them away without hesitation. Not that these older medicines will make you any sicker—they just won't give you the relief that you're expecting, so why bother keeping them around?

6. Find containers so that you can store these like items together in an orderly fashion, once you put everything back under the sink. When we were reorganizing our bathroom, my husband used old shoeboxes that he labeled as such: tooth care (extra toothbrushes, toothpaste, floss, and the like), wound care (bandages, antibiotic creams, and more), girls' stuff (tampons, sanitary pads, and any feminine care products), and so on for anything that we would store in our bathroom.

Too Many Toiletries?

Clutter always gets worse when we bring home free stuff. When it comes to bathrooms, those free toiletries that you can take from hotel rooms are huge culprits. I know that anytime our family travels or when my husband or I travel alone on business, we always load up on the free bottles of shampoo, conditioner, and lotion, along with the bars of soap. I mean, they're free so why not take them home to use? Only problem is that when we emptied our suitcases, we usually would just dump the extra toiletries under the bathroom sink—because, like with many things in our bathroom, we didn't have a defined home for anything so it was the old dump-and-run!

As part of my get-my-bathroom-organized New Year's resolution one year, I decided to finally get those free toiletries organized. I took clear, Rubbermaid bins that were small enough to fit in the space under the sink but big enough to hold these toiletries, and I labeled them according to what I was putting inside them: lotion, soap, shampoo, and conditioner. Then, like a sorting game, I put the toiletries where they belonged. Because I had room left in the bins I'd chosen to use, I added in any full-sized bars of soap and bottles of lotion, shampoo, and conditioner that I'd previously stocked upon in the traditional manner—by buying them at the store. In no time flat I had all of these personal-care products stored in a neat-and-orderly fashion, and the storage area under my sink looked a million times better.

If you travel so much that you've got hundreds and hundreds of bottles of toiletries, you may be able to make some money for your stash. I know plenty of people who put together "care packages" filled with these mini toiletries that they sell at yard sales (remember Constance's "Cashing In" story in Chapter 1?). You may only make a couple of bucks, but if you don't have the space to keep these freebies around, it's better to clear out the clutter than continue to live among it.

Less Clutter, Less Cleaning

One of the biggest benefits of decluttering your bathroom and making it easier to neaten up is that it's also easier to clean it when the time comes. I remember that when we were paying for a cleaning lady, preparing for her arrival meant lots of work the night before. We didn't actually scrub any dirt for her, though: Instead, we were spending hours clearing away the clutter that would be in her way when she got down to cleaning the horizontal surfaces. We were paying good money to worry and fret about clutter, and the real problem was hiding underneath the clean counters.

Even after we no longer wanted to pay to have someone clean our house, the cleaning we did ourselves was always a massive production because we were still dealing with our clutter problem.

Instead of just taking out some bathroom cleaner and a rag, and wiping down the bathroom in ten minutes flat, we would have to spend twice that amount of time getting everything off the countertops and the floor so we could expose the surfaces we needed to clean. Once we got rid of the clutter, the actual act of cleaning became faster and easier to do—and the neat environment we were enjoying encouraged us to keep it neat and to clean it more often.

Here's a great bathroom goal: be able to whip your bathroom into a clean state in fifteen minutes or less. Clearing out the clutter will help tremendously in this regard, because you won't have to pick it up before you can clean the bathroom anymore. You know what else will help? Always having cleaning supplies on hand.

I'm a huge proponent of having cleaning supplies in *each* bathroom of my house. This usually involves a bottle of spray cleaner and rags that I keep under the sink so that when I need to clean a bathroom, I don't need to go anywhere to get my cleaning supplies—

a waste of time, in my mind. Instead, I just reach under the sink, get the supplies I need out, and get the job done. Less than fifteen minutes later, the job *is* done, and I can cross cleaning the bathroom off my mental checklist.

Quick Clutter Challenge

Americans spend about $7 billion each year on personal-care products. While that total number isn't coming out of your pocket alone, I'll bet that your personal-care product spending may be higher than it has to be. Remember the duplicates you bought after the dump-and-run maneuver? Some things may have migrated out of the bathroom over the course of time, as well. Are your daughters' hair ties hiding on dressers? Did the tweezers make their way to the first-aid kit? Is your favorite lotion still in a suitcase after your last trip?

For this chapter's Quick Clutter Challenge, hunt for those products your family needs on a regular basis. Getting them all in one place will save you money in the long run. So set your timer for fifteen minutes and—ready, set, go—find those personal-care products and bring them back to the bathroom where they belong.

Organizing Dirty Laundry

Later on, in Chapter 7: Decluttering the Laundry Room, Garage, Basement, and Attic, I offer in-depth advice on taming the dirty-laundry tiger. But since dirty laundry is often a bathroom clutter problem—it is in my house, at least—I'd like to take a few paragraphs and help you to figure out how best to work through that special kind of stinky clutter.

For starters, what does your family do with their clothes when they get undressed for a shower or bath? Do they get ready in their respective rooms, which have hampers in them, and then wear a robe to and from the shower? Or do they get undressed in the bathroom? My family does the latter so dirty clothes end up there, even though hampers were elsewhere.

Before we got a bathroom hamper—such an obvious solution that seemed to elude us—those dirty clothes were scattered all over the bathroom floor. These days there is always a laundry basket in the bathroom where people can dump their dirty clothes.

Additionally, as a way to cut down on the amount of laundry we have to do in general, I have trained my family not to toss clothing in the laundry after one wearing. Unless the item is visibly soiled or smelly, I've asked everyone to get at least one more wearing out of those clothes. This may seem gross to people not used to this approach, but here's the truth: Clothes last longer when you wash them less. So our practice of wearing jeans two or three times before throwing them in the laundry not only results in our having to do laundry less often but also allows us to keep our clothes longer because they take longer to wear out.

What does this have to do with the clutter problem in the bathroom? Well, before we got it organized, clothes that could be worn again would end up in the pile on the floor with the dirty stuff that really needed to be washed. Not anymore. In addition to the laundry basket to collect dirty clothes, my husband put up a pegboard where people could hang up anything that was worthy of wearing again. I'll admit that this doesn't make for the neatest look in the bathroom—with bras, jeans, and sweatshirts hanging up here and there—but at least everything is up off the floor, and everyone knows where to put the clothes they want to wear again. When they're ready to grab them for the day's outfit, they know where to find those second-time-around clothes.

Ten Tools to Organize Your Bathroom

Looking for additional ways to get your bathroom in order? Here are ten organizational tools for you to try:

1. Pegboard to hang up jewelry, hair dryers, lingerie, and more

2. Flatware organizer to hold makeup tools, toothbrushes, and hair accessories

3. Baskets to store rolled towels and rolls of toilet paper

4. Plastic, stackable bins—these can contain anything that fits inside

5. Hanging shoe organizer for each person's personal-care products

6. Empty paper towel roll to hold hair elastics

7. Strands of ribbons for attaching barrettes and bobby pins

8. Shower caddy with shampoo, conditioner, soap, and shaving supplies for each person to bring into the shower—it'll be just like college!

9. Decorative bowl (from the dining room perhaps) to hold cotton swabs, cotton balls, or other like items

10. Mesh lingerie washing bag for soft things or those that need to drip dry, such as a child's bath toys

Total Cash Back in This Chapter

I have to admit that getting your bathroom organized isn't a huge moneymaker. Perhaps because of the very personal nature of the products you use when primping or cleaning up, there isn't a huge resale market for the clutter you mind find here. That said, there are a few small money-saving opportunities that you might find under the bathroom sink.

Once you get your free toiletries organized and in a place where you can use them on a regular basis, these freebies can go a long way toward saving you some money on soap, lotion, shampoo,

TOSS   KEEP   SELL

TOSS	KEEP	SELL
Old hair-styling tools that are broken	Hair dryer, curling iron, and flat iron that people use on a regular basis	Any extra hair-styling tools you no longer want or need—hair crimper anyone?
Ratty towels (or, turn them into rags or donate them to an animal shelter)	Two bath towels per person per bathroom	Towels you no longer need or want, or which you picked up on sale or got as a gift and have never used
Expired medications and personal-care products, such as sun block	Personal-care products your family uses	Sample sizes of toiletries you may have received as a "free with purchase" or from a hotel, if you can package in a nice way and sell at a yard sale

and conditioner—products you are likely buying for your family anyway. In fact, I was able to go six months without having to buy any shampoo or conditioner for my family after I'd organized all of these sample-sized containers I'd picked up over the years from all of my hotel stays. A year later, we're still washing off with the soap stash. This may have saved me only a few dollars in the long run but I'll take those savings wherever I can find them. Plus, once you get your full-sized bathroom products organized, you'll never again have to spend unnecessary money on duplicates you don't need.

Add those money-savings tactics to a more efficient laundry schedule and the time you'll save when you no longer need to declutter before you clean, and the benefits of a tidy and organized bathroom will keep the rest of the house running smoothly!

Total Cash Back in This Chapter:
$0

chapter 5

CALMING THE CHAOS IN YOUR KITCHEN

I never fully appreciated what it would feel like living in a clutter-free kitchen until my husband and I decided to sell our first house. If you've ever had your home on the market, then you know the machinations you have to go through to get your home to be "show ready."

As far as the kitchen goes, this involves clearing out a ton of the clutter—both out in the open as well as inside the cabinets. Your countertops are supposed to be free of nearly everything (I drew the line at my coffee maker), and your drawers, cabinets, and pantry are supposed to be thinned to the bare minimum. You want to give the impression of wide-open spaces and huge amounts of storage, and homeowners who declutter their home—including their kitchen—usually succeed at giving this impression and helping to make their home sell faster.

Trying to Embrace Your Inner Clutter-Free Kitchen

Once the house sold and we moved into our new place, I tried to continue the show-ready state of our home, but it just didn't work. There were a couple of obstacles standing in my way. First, we'd boxed up so much of our stuff during that sell-the-house period that, once we unpacked it all again after the move, I realized there was just too much in the kitchen to begin with to keep it clutter free at all times. Add to that the fact that our new house had a smaller kitchen with less storage space, so the countertop clutter seemed to have multiplied by the time we'd unpacked all of the boxes and settled in. Finally, without the threat of a last-minute showing always hanging over our head, the impetus to keep the kitchen neat and tidy simply faded away. Soon enough we were back to our cluttered kitchen and feeling like we were living in chaos whenever we needed to cook a meal or get something to eat. I longed for those show-ready days, so slowly I worked my way back to them. There weren't any more showings to worry about, but at least when I was done, I lived in a house a real estate agent would be proud to show any day of the week. I want you to feel that same calmness in your kitchen once you get rid of all of your clutter and chaos.

Cashing In
Dana, Washington, D.C.

I discovered a few years ago that I could help defray the cost of a new washer and dryer by selling the old one on Craigslist. So when my husband and I decided to redo our kitchen, we figured we could help reduce the cost of new appliances by selling our old ones. They all still worked beautifully—they just didn't go with the new look we were going for in the renovated kitchen (they were all white and we were upgrading to stainless steel).

I gave each of the appliances a good scrubbing, took pictures, and posted those pictures on Craigslist. I wrote a detailed ad for each, and because I'd kept all the original paperwork from these appliances, I could include information about them that I might not have known (having that paperwork would become a huge selling point, too). Also, since people always ask if something comes from a smoke-free or pet-free home, I included that, too.

With Craigslist, if something is going to move, it's going to move quickly. You can't post your ad on Monday and then not check your e-mail until Thursday. Also, a Craigslist ad can go stale in a day. So you may have to repost after a few days so you can bump yourself to the top.

Interestingly, the people who ended up responding were land-lords who were looking for inexpensive appliances they could use as upgrades in their rental units. As you know with Craigslist, it's first come, first served, so I didn't haggle too much on price. If someone made an appointment, showed up, and offered me cash, I took it.

These were all Kenmore appliances from the late 1990s, and we ended up selling the refrigerator, the oven/range, and the oven hood to the same person. He offered $400. To me it was a real steal. Plus, I didn't have to pay someone to cart away my appliances (some stores will charge you a fee to take away the old appliances when you buy new), and I didn't have to pay to take them to the dump. At the end of the day, it was really a great deal for both me and the buyer. If someone else can use something and I can make money, that's a big win-win in my book.

We also sold unwanted sunroom furniture on Craigslist. I asked $250 for it, but I got $200. That was awesome because I'd originally purchased it on clearance from Target for $175 and because my husband had wanted to just put it on the curb, hoping someone would take it. It really does pay to take a little more time to sell furniture online before giving up on it entirely!

HOW TO KEEP YOUR COUNTERS CLEAR AT ALL TIMES

There are two tricks to keeping your counters clear and clean:

O Only put out on your counters items that you can't store elsewhere or that you use so regularly it doesn't make sense to put them away after every use.

O Always clear off and wipe down your counters every night before you go to bed so you start the next day with a clean slate—or granite, as the case may be.

As far as the first trick goes, I can justify keeping two appliances on my counter at all times: the coffee maker and the toaster. I use both to make my breakfast every morning so it seems logical to keep them out. But everything else has a permanent home somewhere. This includes the sugar bowl, coffee mugs, and countertop appliances I might use to make dinner, such as the Crock-Pot, slow cooker, or indoor grill. At the same time you won't find my wooden spoons, spatulas, and ladles out on my counter either.

If you don't have places to store the things that are currently taking up space on your counters, you need to find some. Are there cabinets in your kitchen where you're not using the storage space optimally? Can you shift some things around or figure out ways to use risers or dividers in your cabinets so you can make room for the stuff that's cluttering your countertops? Are there items that you use so rarely that you should move them out of the kitchen altogether?

For example, I have a KitchenAid mixer—one of those big pieces that stands about two-feet tall and weighs about twenty pounds. For a long time it sat on the countertop, collecting dust, because I had no place to put it even though I only used it during the winter when I tend to bake a lot. Eventually my husband built shelves in our pantry closet (previously it was just a big open space, with lots of stuff piled on the floor), which quadrupled our storage space. He did one set of shelves deep enough and with enough vertical space to store big countertop appliances like the mixer, which is exactly where we ended up storing it.

The second trick—always clearing off your countertops at night before you go to bed—is important because it prevents your clutter from compounding. You let one day go by without cleaning off the counters and I'm telling you that by day two, you won't have any room left. By staying on top of the clutter problem by tackling it every day, you go a long way toward keeping your kitchen as neat as possible. Plus, I know from firsthand experience what a great feeling it is to wake up in the morning, go downstairs to start the coffee, and have a clutter-free kitchen greet me rather than dishes piled in the sink and yesterday's plates piled on the counter, putting me in a foul mood to start off my morning.

Like bees to honey, clutter attracts more clutter—whether it be the appliances you never bother to put away or the daily dishes you don't make an effort to clean up before you turn in for the night. By keeping your countertops free and clear from clutter as much as you can, you should be able to stop the clutter from multiplying. And then finally you will have that clutter-free kitchen you've always dreamed of having.

DISHING ON HOW TO NEATEN YOUR DISHES, GLASSES, AND FLATWARE

Let's start with some basic calculations. How many place settings of dishes and flatware do you have? Do you have drinking glasses and coffee mugs to match this amount? This is important because if you have too many dishes, not enough forks to match your spoons, or way more drinking glasses than you'll ever need, then it's going to be a real challenge organizing your everyday dishes, glasses, and flatware. This is because you'll have mismatched numbers that may make it difficult for you to serve a meal—and clean up from it, too—in a neat and orderly fashion.

It's ideal to have between eight and twelve place settings of the dishes, glasses, and flatware that you use regularly. This makes it easier for you to arrange shelving so that you can stack dishes and bowls in a single tower, keep your glasses and mugs on a single shelf, and limit your flatware to one sectioned tray in a drawer. To me this is the ultimate in a neat and tidy kitchen.

Do you have way more everyday kitchen pieces than you need? Then it's time to thin the ranks. Clearly, if you have a matched set of dishes—dinner plate, salad plate, bowl, teacup, and saucer— I don't want you breaking up those sets. But what about everything else? We need to do an honest inventory. Our goal is to get your cabinets to look like something you might find in a magazine, and to do that we need to whittle down what's in there. This way when you open a door, you don't have to duck to avoid the things falling out on you.

Here are some things you can immediately pull from your cabinets and drawers to put in either the toss or sell pile:

○ Plastic cups—either freebies from restaurants or baseball stadiums, or those that belong in a picnic basket

○ Drinking or wine glasses if you no longer have enough matching pieces to set a table

○ Any plate, bowl, or cup with a chip or crack in it, or that is worn beyond its prime

○ Sippy cups or other items no longer age-appropriate for your kids

○ Place settings of special-occasion dishes if you do not have enough to use at a dinner party

○ Dishes or cups that no longer reflect your tastes, such as espresso cups (if you gave up coffee) or fondue forks (if you don't have a fondue maker anymore)

Just getting these castoffs out of your cabinets and drawers will help to open up space.

Cashing In
Leslie, California

My china sat in my kitchen closet for years, in a box I'd purchased years ago to keep the china safe. A few years ago a relative died and I inherited her china, and you know what? I liked her china better than my own. So I decided to sell my old china.

I ended up using eBay because I didn't want to give half my profits to a consignment shop, I wasn't interested in having a yard sale, and I didn't want to deal with people coming to my home through a Craigslist ad. In the end my china sold for $10 a place setting.

HOW TO STREAMLINE YOUR ORGANIZATION

Many people I know like to cluster things together in their kitchen, as part of their organizational scheme, based on how those items are used together. For example, where you keep your coffee maker—on your countertop or inside a cabinet—is where you would keep all your coffee-making supplies: coffee to brew, sweetener, filter, mugs, and more. You can use this approach for breakfast cereals—storing the boxes, bowls, and spoons together—but you'd have to draw the line at milk, unless you get the kind that doesn't need refrigeration.

I like to do this with lunch-making supplies. I have one deep drawer in our kitchen that has the lunchboxes, reusable containers for snack packing, refillable water bottles, and any other container I need to pack lunches. The cabinet above is stacked with non-perishables that I buy specifically for packing in lunches.

You can use this approach with other tasks in the kitchen, specifically when you load the dishwasher. Ever since I started grouping things together *inside* the dishwasher, I've been able to unload the dishwasher in about two minutes flat. Even my kids don't complain about doing this task these days. In one handful they can grab all the clean teaspoons (because they were loaded together in the dishwasher when they were dirty). In the next handful they get the forks (again, they were loaded together), and so on with the plates, mugs, cups, and more.

FINDING STORAGE SPACE IN UNLIKELY PLACES

Even if you don't have a kitchen worthy of being on a home design television show—you know, the ones with cabinets galore—you can find plenty of extra storage space if you take a creative look at your kitchen. Here are some ways to eke out extra storage, even in the smallest kitchen:

○ Hang wooden spoons and ladles on the inside of cabinet doors

○ Install hooks underneath hanging cabinets to store coffee mugs

○ Find skinny vertical spaces to keep baking sheets and cutting boards

○ Place dishes and bowls in drawers if overhead cabinet space is at a premium

○ Hang pots and pans from a pot rack

○ Create a bulletin board that you can use to hang kitchen essentials

DO YOU USE ALL YOUR UTENSILS?

Recently, I read in a magazine about a trick you can use to thin your utensil collection. It works in a similar way to the "hangers in the closet" trick I talk about in Chapter 6, Making Sense of the Master and Other Bedrooms. The idea is to get a box, bowl, or basket, and dump all of your utensils in it. Then, as you use and wash these utensils, you put them away in their designated drawers or cabinet space. If you need to use something that you've already used, take it from its place, use it, wash it, and put it back in its designated spot.

At the end of a month, you're supposed to look in the container that once held all of your utensils and see what is left. Ideally, you can determine in one fell swoop that the leftover utensils are those that you truly do not need anymore and you can get rid of them with your mind free and clear.

My only caveat to this would be if you happen to have season-specific utensils that might be in that container and you clearly don't need them because there is no opportunity at that time of the year. I'm thinking, for example, that if you only grill in the summer or only use a carving knife in the winter at Christmas, then your grilling tools and your carving knife will logically be left behind. Therefore, you should try this utensils-in-the-container-trick with these seasonal exceptions in mind. Otherwise, it's an excellent exercise in weeding out what you really don't need to store in your kitchen anymore, and what you can toss in the trash, donate to a good cause, or sell for cash.

PLAY MATCHMAKER IN YOUR KITCHEN

While that old saying of the fastest way to a man's heart is through his stomach seems apropos for a kitchen chapter, when I talk about matchmaking here, I mean this: Your next task in decluttering your kitchen is to match up all the mismatched pieces in your kitchen with their mates. Why? Because once you figure out that you've been storing half a blender or pieces from a food processor you gave away years ago, you can let those pieces go as well and end up with fewer pieces in your kitchen cabinets overall.

The easiest place to start is with your pots and pans. Take them all out and find the tops that go with them. With anything else that comes with more than one piece, find its mate, too.

For example, do you have a spring pan for making cheesecakes—but you lost the bottom years ago? There's no reason to hold onto the spring part of it, since you can't actually bake anything with it if you don't have the bottom. You probably haven't baked a cheesecake in a while, and you won't until you get the missing piece by buying a replacement or getting a whole new pan.

Once you've matched up all the pieces that are match-worthy, you can decide what to do with the orphaned items. Some you should toss in the trash; others may be in good enough shape that you can try to sell them for cash.

Next, move on to the containers you use for storing leftovers and packing lunches. How long has it been since you matched up the plastic tops with the plastic bottoms? I know that I prefer to store the tops and bottoms separately because they stack more compactly this way. However, when you get to the point where you're never using a certain container because you can't figure out where the top is, it's time to recycle that container. Or you need to figure out a way to reuse it as an organizational tool, such as those ideas I mentioned in Chapter 1: Organization Tools You Probably Already Own.

Take the same match-up approach with the small appliances that you use in your kitchen, such as coffeemakers, blenders, and mixers. When it was time for me to go through these items in my kitchen, I discovered that while I had *two* bases for electric blenders, I had none of the attachments that went with them, save for one glass container that had a huge crack up the side. Needless to say, this meant that my blenders were all useless. When I was unsuccessful in trying to donate or sell the pieces, I threw them away.

Here's another reason that this exercise in "matchmaking" will help you to declutter your kitchen: You will likely uncover kitchen products that you've been holding onto all these years that still work perfectly fine (unlike my blenders) but no longer make sense for you to own. Two examples of this from my house are a wok I bought in college and a stovetop griddle. Both are designed to work with a gas-fired cook top with an open flame, and I haven't lived in a house with a gas stove in years. So it wasn't hard for me to decide to put both the wok and the griddle in my "to sell" pile.

Finally, once you make the effort to empty out your kitchen cabinets and drawers, I'll bet you'll end up finding things that you forgot you owned, such as the apple peeler and corer that I bought years ago when I was on an apple pie–baking kick. During our move three years ago, I packed it away and couldn't figure out where I'd put it, and as apple season came and went each year, I mourned the loss of that tool. Because it was pretty pricey to begin with, I drew the line at buying a new one. It just meant that there was no apple pie–baking for me. Eventually, as I decluttered and started putting my kitchen back together, I found the apple peeler and corer. I've got it stashed now with all of the small kitchen appliances that I use on an occasional basis, such as the food processor. This way the next time I'm in the mood to bake an apple pie from scratch, I'll know exactly where to look for my apple peeler and corer.

DECLUTTERING YOUR REFRIGERATOR AND FREEZER

It's important to keep in mind that the food in your refrigerator doesn't keep forever. Even items that you freeze so that they don't rot immediately have expiration dates, too. These items need to be

FOOD STORAGE DEADLINES: REFRIGERATOR AND FREEZER

FOOD	TIME IN THE REFRIGERATOR	TIME IN THE FREEZER
Chicken and turkey	One to two days	Nine months to one year
Ground beef or ground turkey	One to two days	Three to four months
Fresh deli meats	Three to five days	One to two months
Hot dogs	One week (open package); two weeks (new package)	One to two months
Bacon	One week	One month
Bread	One week	Three to four months
Milk	Use by expiration date	One month (make sure you empty out a little milk before freezing it in its plastic container to allow extra space for expansion when it freezes)
Cheese	Use by expiration date; if you see mold on hard cheese, you can cut if off and eat the rest	Four to six months (be sure to put cheese in freezer-safe bags first)
Fresh fish	One to two days	Three to six months
Eggs	Four to five days	You can't freeze eggs
Leftovers	Three to four days	Two to three months

used within a certain amount of time, or they're not going to give you the quality food that you expected when you first purchased them.

A great way to get started with decluttering your refrigerator and freezer is to purge any food that is past its prime. I realize that I'm asking you to throw away good money, but to be honest, once you let food sit around for too long, you've already thrown away good money. I'm just encouraging you to actually put the stuff in the trash.

The Food Storage Deadlines chart is a brief rundown on how long certain foods last in the refrigerator and the freezer. This will allow you to plan accordingly when you go food shopping and make sure that you don't overbuy (thus creating clutter in the fridge) and end up throwing away food that expires before you're able to use it.

Also, keep in mind that from here on in, you should take a marker and write on all of your food packages, in big letters that you'll be able to read through any frost on the package, the "use by" date. You'll write this based on the life spans described in the Food Storage Deadlines chart. Then be sure that you stock your food in the refrigerator or freezer with the oldest stuff toward the front so it's easier for you to find it and use it first.

Taming the Paper Tiger—The Mail

A big part of our kitchen's clutter problem used to come from the mail. I would pick up the mail at the same time I got the kids from school. We'd all walk into the house—and into the kitchen for a snack—where I'd dump the mail. Sometimes I'd sort through it immediately, tossing unwanted items right in the recycle bin, and placing bills in the "bills to be paid" bin we had on the kitchen's bookcase.

Other days, though, we'd rush in, grab a quick snack, and then rush right out to an afterschool activity. Then the mail pile would sit there on the counter, where I might deal with it when I got home or the next day or the day after next. By that point a couple more days' worth of mail had accumulated and, well, you get the picture.

The way to tame the paper tiger that is the daily mail is to deal with it as soon as you get it into your hands. Before you start opening envelopes, position yourself next to your shredder or recycle bin. Then as you go through the mail, you can shred any credit card offers, recycle direct mail you're not interested in keeping (I have a soft spot for shoe catalogs), and then deal with the mail that needs your attention, such as bills to be paid or communication from your kids' school.

That said, I understand that there are certain days when, though your intentions are good, you just don't have the time to deal with every piece of mail. That's why we created a mail bin in our house, which I referenced in Chapter 2, Organizing the Living and Family Rooms. As I mentioned there, we've reused a metal bin that we used to use to chill drinks at our backyard barbecues. Now it's the place where the mail goes when we're running short on sorting time. Professional organizers may shudder at our use of the mail bin, because they profess the "only touch it once" way of organizing your home. And by looking at the mail, then putting it in the mail bin until we have more time to really look at and sort it, we are breaking that "touch it once" rule.

Well, I've tried that rule. Sometimes it worked and sometimes it didn't. And when I couldn't make "touch it once" work, I ended up getting on my own case and feeling guilty that something was wrong with me.

Quick Clutter Challenge

At one time I had way too many pie tins and baking plates. It started with pie tins I owned before I was married. More arrived over the years as I received gifts. I don't run a bakery and could never use the plates I had, but they kept coming anyway and eventually the stack just had to go.

Maybe you have too many of one thing in your kitchen. Do you have a few too many serving spoons? Or a cupboard full of sealable plastic containers—with lids that may not match or fit? Is your silverware drawer just overflowing in general?

Whatever your collection is, it's time to thin it out. Do you know how many you have? Do you actually cook with or use all of them? Do you even know where all of them are? And that's what this chapter's Quick Clutter Challenge is all about. So set your timer for fifteen minutes, and find your kitchen multiples and gather them up so you can sell them. Ready, set, go get your stuff!

There was nothing wrong with *me*, I've come to realize. There is something wrong with that *approach* and how it could work (or not work) for my way of life. I've made my peace with that and moved on.

No one should feel bad about the way she chooses to deal with the stuff in her house, so if you need to create a stop-gap measure like we have with our mail bin, do it. Remember: Having this mail bin accomplishes the clutter busting we're trying to achieve. Thanks to this bin my mail no longer covers surfaces in my house—from the kitchen counters to the living room furniture (as I'd mentioned in Chapter 2). This way the mail is in one, contained place and, for all intents and purposes, is no longer clutter in my kitchen.

 *What's It Worth?*

When it comes to finding rare treasures in the kitchen, Jeff Jeffers of Garth Auctioneers says that it is, indeed, possible. "Kitchen objects tend to come in three categories," he says. The first category is what he calls "country America." Items here would include ornamental iron pieces, such as trivets, metal scoops, and ladles, and knives that have ornamental details on them that show some level of craftsmanship. These items are typically from the eighteenth and nineteenth century.

Next you have kitchen objects from the Victorian era and first half of the twentieth century. Jeffers says that you'll find value in

German stoneware and American utilitarian pieces. Jeffers shares an anecdote to show how valuable something so basic as stoneware really can be.

"I had a fellow bring in a stoneware crock that he'd gotten for $12 at a country auction," recalls Jeffers. "The piece had an incised eagle on it and, sadly, a huge crack in it. Nonetheless, this man had a feeling that it's valuable so he handed over his $12 and brought it to me. This guy had an eye for quality and had made a profit from old tools he'd bought at country auctions in the past. So when he brought this piece of stoneware to me, he asked, 'Do you think you can get enough for it so that I can take my wife out to dinner?' and I told him that I thought I could get him enough to take her out to dinner for five or six years." Because it was a rare piece of stoneware from the Victorian era, Jeffers ended up selling it for $34,000.

Finally, there are mid-century kitchen pieces in which Jeffers says "form dominates." This is the time frame of art deco up through the '50s and '60s, where bright, garish colors were all the rage. "You can certainly find period light fixtures that fall into this modern category," he says.

People who collect from this time period are looking for items with modernist shapes—bullet shapes, space-age looking things. So if you bought an older house and are tearing out all the old appliances and fixtures, you may want to have an appraiser give them a once-over before you list them for practically nothing on Craigslist or, worse, toss them out with your trash.

TOSS	KEEP	SELL
Non-working kitchen appliances or those missing necessary pieces/accessories	Any appliances you use on a regular basis	Redundant kitchen appliances or those that are still working or in good shape that are useless to you in your current kitchen
Rusted out pots and pans	Pots and pans you're still using	Duplicate pots and pans
Chipped, cracked, or worn-out place settings, cups, and flatware	Everyday dishes, cups, and utensils where you still have all the matching pieces	Extra plates, cups, and flatware

Total Cash Back in This Chapter

If you happen to be renovating your kitchen, you can make some big bucks by selling your old appliances to offset the cost of new ones, like Dana did. She took in $400 for things she was going to bring to the dump. Not that I think you should totally redo your kitchen just to get it organized, but selling your appliances is definitely a way to bring in extra cash.

So is putting any duplicates of plates, utensils, or cooking tools up for sale—especially if you haven't used them in a long time.

Remember Leslie's anecdote about china that she'd been holding onto for years? She was able to sell twelve place settings at $10 a pop, bringing in $120 for something useless that she'd been storing for years. What else can you uncover in your kitchen that can bring in extra cash? Did you recently get a new coffeemaker as a gift and have a perfectly good (but older) coffeemaker that you can sell at a yard sale? Do you have mismatched plates, glasses, and utensils that you could put on Craigslist? I'm betting that any nearby college students looking to furnish a first apartment or a frat house would be happy to take these mismatched sets off your hands for a few bucks.

Finally, when it comes to getting cash back in the kitchen, keep in mind how important it is to use all of the food you have. With just a little bit of management, your refrigerator and freezer will be organized and orderly, and you'll use your food in a timely manner so that you're not throwing away money when things go bad.

Total Cash Back in This Chapter: **$520**

chapter 6

MAKING SENSE OF THE MASTER AND OTHER BEDROOMS

There's nothing as pleasant as going into your bedroom to retire for the night, and finding a neat, inviting space. But if you're busy, it's easy to let your bedroom get out of control. And once your bedroom gets messy, falling right to sleep rarely happens. Instead of climbing right into bed, you may be stepping over dirty laundry, sidling by piles of books on the floor, and flinging blankets about to figure out how you are going to transform the mess on top of your bed into something in which you can go to sleep.

In this chapter I'm going to help you make sense of your master bedroom, as well as the other bedrooms in your home, including your kids' rooms and the guest room, if you have one. This should help you to make these rooms neater over time and also to uncover earning opportunities that may be hidden underneath those piles of clean laundry that you never got around to putting away.

Calm the Chaos in Your Closet

How many times have you looked in your clothes closet, saw it teeming with clothing—some hanging up, some on the floor, some hanging on hooks—and thought, "Gee, I've got nothing to wear"? I know I have, and I've since learned that this is a sign that I've got too many pieces of useless clothing.

One of the best ways to get your closet organized—and figure out how to make cash for your clothing—is to thin out the attire you own. You can get started by taking a walk through your closet and identifying clothing that has dust on the shoulders. I know this sounds crazy but clothing can actually get dusty, too. And what should dust on the shoulders say to you? That this article of clothing has been hanging in your closet for so long, unworn, that it's started to collect dust.

I would pull out those dusty pieces, brush them off, and then determine if they are worthy of resale. You can do that by asking yourself these three questions:

1. Are the clothes still in good condition?

2. Do they seem reasonably fashionable?

3. Are they clean and ready to go?

Photo © iStockphoto/vasiliki

If your closet looks like this one, odds are you can't even see all of your clothes—never mind wear them!

I keep a large shopping bag in the bottom of my closet where I can stash clothes I plan to sell or donate to charity. If you don't have a stashing system set up yet, get one going now. We are going to be doing a lot of culling of your clothing.

Cashing In
Michelle, North Carolina

I have always consigned my children's clothing after they've grown out of them. I believe that you can get more money by consigning than you can from having a garage sale. At a garage sale, even children's clothing in really good condition goes for fifty cents or $1.00 an item because people go to garage sales looking for bargains, not gently worn clothes with a bigger price tag.

At a consignment shop, people already know that they will be paying less than they would for brand-new clothing and that they are going to get better quality than something they would find at a garage sale. Because the consignment shop prices things a bit higher, even with their share of the profit, I make more money. I can take home anywhere from $30 to $40 from consigning my kids' clothes. I've been doing this for so long, I have no idea how much money I've taken in over the years, but I'm sure it's a lot.

No drawer is spared when I decide it's time to consign. I pull out everything from the bureaus and closets, and I divide to conquer. There's always a "for sale" pile, but I also set aside things to donate and items to toss.

If something needs to be fixed before I consign it—a button is missing or a jacket needs a new zipper, for example—I don't even bother putting it in a "for sale" pile. I know that I'll never get around to fixing it, and I just want to clear out the clutter. I usually end up donating those items. Clothes too worn or damaged to donate are tossed, right then and there.

It's important to keep in mind when consigning clothes that you are not likely to get what you paid for them, and you're likely to be the only one who ever knows how often it was (or wasn't) worn. Instead, try to think about it as if you were buying these things used and what you would think was a fair price as a buyer. If you wouldn't spend $30 on a used jacket for your son, it's likely the consignment store's clients wouldn't either. You can use your own sense of value as your rule of thumb, and you'll understand the potential your items have better each time you go back. And when the consignment shop makes you an offer that you think is too low, you can always take your stuff and try to sell it on Craigslist.

GET HELP FROM YOUR HANGERS

I know lots of people who hang all of their clothes with the hangers facing one way, and then every time they wear that garment, they turn the hanger the other way when they put it back. At the end of six months, they'll do a walk through of their closet and see how many articles of clothing they never touched—meaning the hangers never changed direction. If you're having trouble figuring out which clothing you can get rid of, because you can't keep track of what you've worn lately, this technique is a surefire way to identify clothes that have fallen out of fashion in your mind—even if you never realized or thought about this before.

DIVIDE BY DRAWERS

Don't have a big closet that you can do the hanger trick with? Then use the drawers in your dresser to try something similar.

No need to reconfigure how you store things in your dresser drawers, but instead designate a few drawers that, from here on in, will be the only active drawers that you use. This is where you will put away your current clothing after you've worn and washed it. After a few weeks of doing this, you should be able to quickly identify what clothing you haven't worn in a while—because it never made it into those "active" drawers.

If you don't have enough dresser space to do this, try this trick with your existing drawer space instead: Stack your neatly folded clothing on one side of your drawers, and then when you wear and wash something, put it back on the other side of the drawer. Again, this will give you an easy way to identify what you never got around to wearing, because those articles of clothing never made it to the other side of the drawer. (You'll find tips in Chapter 10 on how to make money from the clothing you've now identified that you no longer want or need.)

If your kids are still young enough that you're in charge of their dressers, closets, clothing, and laundry, you can use similar hanger and drawer tricks to uncover the clothing that has fallen out of fashion. With older kids I think it's best to sit down with them every three to six months and review their entire wardrobe. I know that when I do this with my own daughters, they can easily tell me which pieces they love and which ones they never want to see again—even though we just bought some of those things new a few months ago. You know how fickle and finicky teens can be about fashion. I know right away what clothing they don't like anymore by how my daughters wrinkle their nose or get a look of disgust on their face when I hold up that piece of clothing.

 ## What's It Worth?

Could a quilt you have laying on your bed be worth big bucks? It's possible, as one woman I interviewed for this book found out. She'd purchased a quilt at a yard sale for $75 and years later decided to have it appraised. Experts told her it was worth $1,000.

Auctioneer Jeff Jeffers of Garth Auctioneers isn't convinced, however. "Even with quilts that have been handed down from generation to generation, the possibility of a quilt breaking out of the $50 to $300 range at auction is often not great," he says. "The quilt market is down today overall."

Jeffers likens this to the fact that today's marketplace is flooded with hand-me-downs from baby-boomer parents, who have all downsized and gotten rid of their stuff. At the same time, buyers in their twenties and thirties are not interested in acquiring folksy things like quilts. "It's Economics 101 of supply and demand," he adds, meaning that there's a huge supply of quilts and not a big demand for them.

That said, there are instances when quilts do bring in big bucks. A Baltimore quilt that someone brought in to *Antiques Roadshow* ended up selling at auction for $15,000. And in February 2010, the *St. Louis Dispatch* reported that a local couple paid $72,700 for two, fifty-year-old quilts that were in perfect condition and featured portraits and signatures from famous baseball players including Hall of Famers.

So if you've got a quilt in your guest bedroom with a likeness of Babe Ruth on it—and his signature as well—you might want to take that to an auction house.

There's Gold in Them Thar Jewelry Boxes!

All those TV commercials telling you that there's never been a better time to cash in on your gold jewelry are right: As of this writing, gold is selling for nearly $1,000 an ounce. That's not to say that your old college class ring will net you that kind of cash, but you might get something for it, beyond years of tarnish. Here are five tips for getting the most money for your gold jewelry:

1. Set aside some time to go through your jewelry box and look for gold pieces. Because gold's value is determined by weight, heavy pins, bracelets, and necklaces are especially valuable when trading in. But that doesn't mean you shouldn't also bring in gold earrings that are on the lighter side. Basically, if the piece is at least 14-karat gold and you don't want it anymore, put it aside for selling.

2. Don't send your gold to any companies that promise to send you a check for your jewelry. Once your stuff is out of your hands, you may never see a dime for it. Instead, find a local jeweler who is offering to buy gold from regular people like you. (I see signs in jewelry store windows all the time, saying "We buy gold!")

3. While the first jeweler you visit may give you a great offer, you might get a better offer somewhere else. Visit two or three local jewelers so you can compare and contrast the offers they make for your gold jewelry.

4. Once someone makes you an offer you can't refuse, don't just hand over your jewelry. Instead, check with your local Better Business Bureau to make sure the jeweler has a clean business record. This is a good way to feel confident that you're doing business with someone you can trust. Nonetheless, always get your offer in writing, in case there are any problems with the transaction.

5. The jeweler will likely ask you for identification before cutting you a check. This helps the jeweler check up on you and make sure you're not a wanted jewel thief.

Hopefully, you'll come home to a decluttered jewelry box with a big fat check for your gold jewelry.

Quick Clutter Challenge

When you get to the heart of consignment, things that hold their value tend to sell for more money. It only makes sense that consignments and jewelers usually pay good prices for more precious items, so this Quick Clutter Challenge will focus on the finding and selling of jewelry.

Now, we all know jewelry should be kept somewhere safe, but there are always reasons it doesn't end up there. Whether you get distracted and leave a bracelet by the sink while you are doing dishes or whether your girls more carelessly leave their earrings on the living room table, you'll likely need to consolidate what you own before you consider selling it. Set your timer for fifteen minutes, find the jewelry you took off and left lying around, and locate matches for any orphaned earrings you may have.

When you're done, you can figure out which pieces are worth keeping and which ones you should have appraised at your local jeweler (if you think they might be worth big bucks) or polished and cleaned to sell on consignment. Some of my Suddenly Frugal blog readers have told me that they've made as much as $600 from selling their jewelry. I'll bet that got your attention. Got your timer set? Then ready, set, go get your jewelry.

Figuring Out Which Furniture You Need

We are lucky that our family has been very generous with us, giving us pieces of furniture for not only our bedroom but also other rooms in the house. But in our bedroom alone, we have at least four items that we did not buy: our two nightstand tables and two of our dressers. That doesn't sound so bad, except those dressers, for example, are in addition to the four dressers that came as built-ins in the master bedroom closet. Every drawer in those dressers is stuffed to the gills, and they take up nearly all the wall space in our bedroom.

What does having all of these dressers tell me?

O   We have too much furniture in our bedroom.

O   We have too much clothing.

What are the chances that this sounds like your bedroom?

Using the tactics mentioned earlier in this chapter for calming the chaos in our closet, I have started to thin out our clothing. Soon enough, I should be able to consign some of my clothing and then sell one or two of those dressers to free up space in my bedroom and to make some extra cash.

The same syndrome of too much clothing and too many dressers is also true in one of my daughter's bedrooms. While she has a generous-sized room for a teenager, she has two larger dressers that are overflowing with clothes, like her mom's and dad's dressers were at one point. There are times, when all her laundry is clean and put away, that she can barely close the drawers. The one caveat I will add to this two-dresser scenario is this: My daughter uses one of those dressers for her off-season clothing. So one dresser has everything she needs for warm weather and the other is for cold weather. Well, at least in theory that's how we set things up. These days I find T-shirts commingling with turtlenecks.

This is why at the end of a season it's always a good idea to review the clothing you own. Got to September and never wore that brand-new bathing suit you got on sale last year? What are the chances you're going to wear it next year? Probably slim to none, which is why you should put that bathing suit in your "to consign" box or bag that you're now keeping at the bottom of your closet or somewhere in your bedroom. What about the bikini you're still holding onto after all these years, in hopes that you'll get back your bikini body? Well, if that bathing suit is in decent shape, why not make some money off of it by bringing it to a resale shop? Look, if you *do* ever get your bikini body back, you can reward yourself with a brand-new bathing suit, not one that's been sitting in a dresser drawer for the last ten years.

At the end of your purge cycle, I bet you'll end up needing fewer pieces of furniture. Then you can clean up that dresser or nightstand that's now unwarranted, take some pictures of it, and upload it to Craigslist or whichever way you would like to sell your castoffs for cash. Best of all, with fewer pieces of furniture in your bedroom, you'll have less to dust.

Cashing In
Dyene, Texas

Recently, I decided to weed out eleven years of accumulated "stuff." I determined that the best way to sell the things I didn't want anymore was through a community classified page online. Neither eBay nor Craigslist have worked out well for me in the past, and having a garage sale was not an option because my neighborhood does not allow them.

I researched everything on the Internet before I set a price and made sure people could tell how much they'd save by buying from me.

Also, I made sure that everything I was selling had been treated well over the years. Really, I'd kept it in nearly perfect condition. And (this is very important) I kept the boxes and owner's manuals of everything I own. This seemed to be a huge selling point. Buyers seemed to appreciate knowing I was careful enough with my things to be that organized and particular.

Also, I was thoughtful about how I wrote my ads. For example, when I was selling my couch, I didn't just write "Couch for sale." I told the buyers why it worked for us, hoping they'd agree: "This sofa is very comfy and the seat reclines (see pic). I wanted design, my husband wanted comfort. This couch was the perfect compromise! In excellent condition." And I got $375 for it!

Here are some examples of things I've sold through the online community classifieds:

O Bed—I bought it for $75, and sold it for $350

O Dining room table—I bought it for $499, and it sold for $525

O Bedroom set—I bought it for $850, and sold it for $1,100

Since I am very frugal, I bought everything I own on sale and I usually turn a profit when I resell it. When you talk up your furniture for sale the right way, people are really willing to give you good money for a good deal in return.

I've also learned not to take the first offer that anyone makes. People often start out offering less than they are actually willing to pay. So if I am selling an item for $75 and someone offers me $50, we'll usually settle somewhere closer to $60 or $65.

All told, I've made about $4,000 selling stuff I didn't need anymore. Best of all, after I'd posted these things to this online community bulletin board, everything sold in less than an hour.

ANTIQUES IN THE ATTIC OR NEXT TO THE BED

If your bedroom furniture pieces are hand-me downs like mine are, there's something you should think about before you go selling your stuff on Craigslist: Might you have a diamond in the rough, an antique piece of furniture that could be worth some serious money? Two things that may show that you have an antique on your hands or, at the very least, a well-made piece of furniture that may be worth a pretty penny: manufacturer labels inside drawers or on the back or underside of cabinets, and solid construction.

Some furniture manufacturers have better reputations than others, so knowing who made your bedroom set or where it was from will help you determine its value and how you should price it when you sell. For example, when researching this chapter, I discovered a metal plate that read "Kling Mayville, New York" inside

Making Your Bed

There is something about making your bed in the morning that inspires you to keep the rest of your room neat. Who knows the psychology behind it? All I can tell you is that it works. So as you slowly move toward getting your bedroom in order and finding castoffs you can cash in, try to make time to make your bed every day. It doesn't have to be perfectly made, with lots of decorative pillows—just neat enough that if feels made to you and makes you feel good when you walk into your bedroom and see it.

the top drawer of a dresser my in-laws once owned. I learned that this upstate New York furniture maker, which Ethan Allen bought in the early 1960s, went out of business about ten years ago. The cherry bedroom set I have was originally made in the late 1950s, before Ethan Allen took over. While I couldn't determine the value of the furniture itself, the drawer hardware alone is somewhat valuable. Some furniture historians will pay $5 to $15 *per drawer pull* from these sets. Between the one dresser and two nightstands, there are sixteen handles, or $80 to $240 in potential income. I've never been a big fan of the drawer pulls anyway, so I'm considering removing them for cash, and then replacing them with something I like more.

Solid construction, though, can be just as important. Newer furniture comes with the drawers glued together; older, more solid pieces of furniture feature dovetailing inside drawers. This is like a checkerboard that you would see behind the drawer face, where the two pieces of wood come together like a puzzle. This signifies good construction. Even better are dovetailed drawers that seem to have been hand carved, meaning the lines and boxes aren't uniform in shape. This usually is the mark of an older piece of furniture, which could be more valuable.

If you figure out that you might have some antiques worthy of real money, I would recommend getting them appraised. You can wait until your local auction house or art gallery has a free appraisal day, and then bring in one of your pieces. You can make an appointment at your local auction house or art gallery; appraisal should always be free. Or, if you're looking for an appraisal *and* your fifteen minutes of fame, you could try to get yourself on the PBS show *Antiques Roadshow*. Visit *www.pbs.org* for more information on getting tickets to have your stuff appraised on TV.

Putting Everything in Its Place

Has your nightstand become a catchall for anything you may have brought with you into your bedroom? I know that in the past mine was. Which is why if you were to have opened one of my nightstand drawers, you would have found sleep-related stuff (eye mask and ear plugs, for example) along with other items that would have left me scratching my head. I mean, just how did a ten-year-old tube of lipstick, a deck of cards, and a stapler end up in there?

My guess is somewhere along the line I was cleaning out some old boxes or a suitcase, or working on a project that required stapling, and I ran out of time. And rather than bring each of those items back to where they belonged—deck of cards into the kids' playroom, the stapler back to my office, and that old lipstick to the trash—I just dumped them in that drawer, closed it, and forgot about the stuff.

While I'm using my nightstand as an example of why you should put everything in its place, this advice really applies to any room in your house. My guess is if you've got a dump-and-run approach to cleaning, as I used to have, your drawers, cabinets, and closets contain a mish-mosh of things that belong somewhere else.

Starting today I want you to dedicate one fifteen-minute period toward tackling one drawer or one cabinet in your bedroom and elsewhere in your house. See if you can't start making progress toward getting everything back in its original place. In the process you'll be decluttering things and identifying the stuff that you can eventually sell.

You'll also be saving yourself money. Let's use my example again. Remember that deck of cards? Well, when I found it way back when, immediately I went outside and put it in the car. Why? We have carriers in the back seats where the kids can store their entertainment for road trips. So now the next time we head out on a vacation or road trip, I'll know that when my kids ask to play a game of Spit, I won't have to spend extra money buying a deck of cards at the local pharmacy—I'll already have one ready to go in the car.

Cashing In
Jen, New Jersey

I've bought clothes on eBay, so I figured why couldn't I sell my stuff there, too? For example, last year I bought this wonderful pair of patent leather heels that I thought for sure I'd wear over the summer. But then spring, summer, and fall went by, and I never got around to wearing them. So I put them up for sale, as new-in-box, on eBay, and they sold instantly for $20.

The same thing happened with a pair of running shoes that didn't work out for me. I'd already run in them a few times, and I couldn't return them. So after they sat in my room for nine months, I sold them. Runners are very loyal to shoes, and some will buy a barely used pair. I paid $90 for them new, but sold them for only $18.50.

I always use two or three pictures when selling shoes on eBay. It's worth the extra cost because, as a consumer, I know I wouldn't buy something without seeing a few pictures of the item first.

With both pairs of shoes, I didn't mind that I didn't make a lot of money on the sales. I was never going to use them, and they were just taking up space in my room. So why not get a few bucks for them?

Coin Counting

Another hazard in a bedroom is spare change. Many people carry around loose coins in their pockets, only to empty those pockets when they undress for the day and get into their pajamas. Unless they have a designated spot for putting change, it can end up all over the place—on dresser tops, inside drawers, and on the floor. You may find that your kids have the same loosey-goosey approach to their cash and may have their allowance scattered all over the floor of their rooms.

Unless you've done it in the past few months, it's probably about time you counted up all that spare change. This will give you or your kids extra spending money the next time you need to buy something, and you just might be surprised at how much money you turn up. Then, from there on in, designate a specific spot in your bedroom where you can empty your pockets. In our bedroom that spot is a small basket on a dresser.

Even with our spare-change spot, it's important to clear it out on a regular basis so it doesn't end up overflowing and so you can put some cash in your wallet. I usually do a coin counting every other month, and recently when I counted out the change, here's what we ended up with:

- four single bills or $4
- four "gold" dollars or $4
- thirty-seven quarters or $9.25
- twenty-four dimes or $2.40
- fifteen nickels or $.75
- fifty pennies or $.50
- fifty cents Euro

All told this adds up to nearly $21. While I didn't earn this money in the traditional sense of selling my clutter for cash, this is a significant amount that's worth mentioning. Again, I tend to add up our spare change once every other month, which means that, on average, I'm collecting $10 a month or $120 a year in spare change. If your spare change habits are anything like mine, then you'll definitely want to designate a spot for spare change in your bedroom and then cash it in on a regular basis like I do.

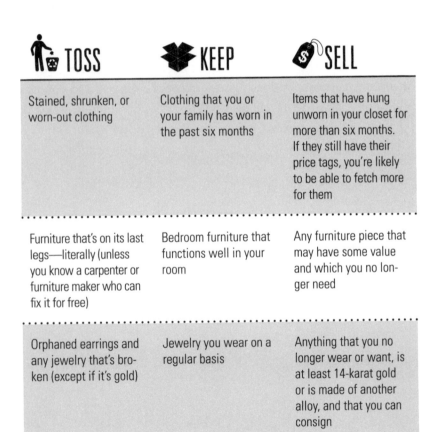

TOSS	KEEP	SELL
Stained, shrunken, or worn-out clothing	Clothing that you or your family has worn in the past six months	Items that have hung unworn in your closet for more than six months. If they still have their price tags, you're likely to be able to fetch more for them
Furniture that's on its last legs—literally (unless you know a carpenter or furniture maker who can fix it for free)	Bedroom furniture that functions well in your room	Any furniture piece that may have some value and which you no longer need
Orphaned earrings and any jewelry that's broken (except if it's gold)	Jewelry you wear on a regular basis	Anything that you no longer wear or want, is at least 14-karat gold or is made of another alloy, and that you can consign

Total Cash Back in This Chapter

I love settling in for the night in a neat and tidy bedroom, one where my clothes aren't spilling out of my dresser drawers and my walls aren't crowded with extra furniture. This chapter gave you all the tools you'll need to minimize what you own while helping you to identify which things in your bedroom—and bedroom closet—could bring in extra cash. From selling your gold jewelry to making money from a vintage bedroom set to scooping up loose change, you should understand now what a treasure trove your bedroom could be.

Total Cash Back in This Chapter: $4,960

chapter 7

DECLUTTERING THE LAUNDRY ROOM, GARAGE, BASEMENT, AND ATTIC

While every room in a cluttered house has the potential to be messy, the areas in which you are most likely not entertaining on a regular basis—but rather storing stuff—are the rooms where the clutter is the worst. I'm talking specifically about the laundry room, garage, basement, and attic. In many of these rooms of the house, you may have an "out of sight, out of mind" mindset about your mess—meaning that if you're not seeing it or dealing with it on a daily basis, you're not admitting that there is a mess going on there.

I know that was how I used to think, until I realized how much easier my daily living would be once I got these secondary areas of my home in order. So in this chapter I'm going to give you step-by-step instructions for decluttering your laundry room, garage, basement, and attic and, trust me, you'll be thankful that you did.

Organizing Your Laundry Room

My mom is the master of laundry—always has been, probably always will be. She knew how to keep a laundry room neat and tidy, and I'm embarrassed that, despite all those years spent growing up in her house, I never picked up any of her laundry-room skills. No matter where she's lived, my mom has had a table in her laundry room for folding clothes, a line for hanging up delicates, and a shelving system for holding laundry supplies. In addition, she always had a sorting system so that the dreaded red sock never ended up in the white load of laundry, thus creating a pile of pink clothes.

Now my mother has always been lucky enough to have enough *space* in each of her homes for her neat-and-tidy laundry center. So my excuse for why my laundry room was always a disaster always hinged on the fact that I believed I didn't have enough space to do what I needed to get done in my laundry room. Well, no more excuses.

In this section I'm going to help you figure out the best way to use whatever laundry room you have—even if you don't have one.

For example, in one house where we lived, the so-called laundry room was actually in the kitchen—a washer and dryer tucked into a closet near the eat-in area. Maybe your laundry set up sounds like that and you feel hopeless about getting it in order and keeping it that way. Please don't. With a little bit of practice and a lot of patience (for yourself), you can eventually have a neat and tidy laundry room and keep it that way. Plus, when all the laundry is done, you'll have a better sense of what castoff (yet clean) clothing you are no longer interested in keeping and therefore can sell for cash. (See Chapter 10, Selling Your Stuff for Cash for tips on figuring out which articles of clothing you should consign and which you should take to a resale shop for cash upfront.)

Let's start by asking some questions of ourselves that can help us to uncover the roadblocks we've set up that are preventing us from having a neat and tidy laundry room.

WHAT IS ACTUALLY IN YOUR LAUNDRY ROOM?

When you ask yourself that question, what's your answer? Besides the dirty and clean laundry and the laundry detergent, are there non-laundry things that are cluttering your laundry room and preventing you from using the space optimally? I can tell you that, at one time, you would find things as varied as shoe polish and shampoo in my laundry room. Why? Because there was open shelving in that laundry room, which happened to be adjacent to the master bathroom and bedroom—places where someone might need some shampoo or, when getting dressed in the morning, might need to shine his shoes.

Clearing out items that don't belong in your laundry room to begin with can leave you with a more organized space.

Photo © iStockphoto/chandlerphoto

Here's the problem with that storage scenario: Those non-laundry items were taking up precious real estate that, when filled, left things overflowing onto the floor. For example, with shampoo and shoe polish cluttering the shelves in my laundry room, I would be left to balance the detergent on the side of the washing machine, and it would always end up on the floor during the spin cycle. Once I recognized my clutter culprits, I found new homes for those non-laundry items somewhere else—shoe polish near my shoes in the closet, and shampoo stored under the bathroom sink with like toiletries. Then, I was able to stack the laundry detergent and other laundry supplies up and off the floor or the side of the appliances, and give myself more room to move around.

DO YOU HAVE SUFFICIENT SHELVING OR STORAGE IN YOUR LAUNDRY ROOM?

If you don't yet have shelves, cabinets, or bins in your laundry room, this could be as big a part of your problem as storing non-laundry items in the space that should be used for laundry supplies. Putting up shelves, at the very least, is an easy solution that even a would-be handyman with two thumbs could handle. You may even be able to find shelving supplies stashed somewhere in the house—basement, garage, or shed. Really, all you need is a few pieces of wood, some brackets, and screws.

Not interested in putting up shelves? Well, can you get a free-standing bookcase in there or at least some bins in which you can put your laundry supplies so that they're not spilling out all over the room? The idea here is to make sure that whatever you need to successfully do your laundry is easily stored in your laundry room so you quite literally have it at your fingertips whenever you need to throw in a load of laundry.

Try some of these ideas to make the most of your laundry room space so you can maximize its use and keep it neat at the same time:

O Carve out a notch or area where you can stash a folding card table and ironing board so you always have a flat surface for taking care of clean clothes that need folding or ironing. When you're not using them, you fold them up and slip them into their vertical notch. I imagine that together they wouldn't take up more than a foot of space across.

O If you like to keep a variety of baskets or bins in the laundry room for sorting, can you create a series of shelves into which you can slip those baskets or bins— and therefore get them off the floor? Or, do you have a cabinet or shelving unit with slide-out shelves that can become your de facto sorting areas? At the very least, maybe you can invest in mesh laundry bins that fold flat (like the table and ironing board mentioned above) so that when you don't need them for sorting, you can fold them flat and stash them away in a small space.

O Do you have a front-loader washing machine and matching dryer? If so, maybe you should invest in those pedestals that are meant to act as bases for these machines and in which you can store all your laundry supplies. True, they cost about $200 each but if space is limited in your laundry room and you're

really looking to cut down on the clutter, this may
be the best $400 you ever spend toward a neater
laundry room.

WHERE DO PEOPLE PUT THEIR DIRTY CLOTHES AT THE END OF THE DAY?

In the house I grew up in, our hamper was in the bathroom,
under the sink. Since our house was very small, as was the single bathroom in the house, we didn't have any room to spare for
a laundry basket in there. So using that area under the sink was
ingenious. When it was full, it was time to do the laundry.

In our house now, unfortunately, we have many places where
people put their dirty laundry—in their respective bedrooms, in
the bathroom where the shower is, and on the floor of the laundry
room. To be fair the house in which I grew up had only two people in it—my mother and me. Now I live in a family of four, with
two kids who play sports (read: lots of sweaty, smelly clothes to
wash on a daily basis). This means there is twice as much laundry
to be done—if not triple or quadruple the normal amount. Add
to that the haphazard places that people put their dirty laundry,
and it's no wonder our laundry room is often declared a disaster
zone—or at least it used to be.

Do you have similar disorder in your house when it comes to
where people put their dirty laundry? If so, you've got to stop the
insanity. Take a page from my mom's single-hamper approach to
laundry, and try that in your house. Designate one place where
people put their dirty laundry. This could be a laundry basket in
each person's room, with the explicit understanding that when

said basket is full, that person will throw in a load of his or her own laundry. Or, it could be a communal laundry basket in the laundry room. Then, when it's full, you know it's time to start a load of laundry. You may even have to establish a hard-core rule that "if it's not in the designated laundry basket, it's not getting washed" to make the message sink in for your family. Once you've established the go-to place for dirty laundry, it should help stop the chaos on the floor of your laundry room.

HOW OFTEN DO YOU DO LAUNDRY AND PUT IT AWAY?

There's a certain irony to how our family used to handle laundry in our house. We had no problem washing the laundry; putting it away was where we got stuck. Why the disconnect? I'm not sure. But here's what usually happened.

Someone would announce that he or she was out of clean underwear or socks, or that there weren't any clean jeans left to wear to school. So I would wash a load of laundry, pull it out of the washer, and put it in the dryer. Then, I would start another load, pull the dry stuff out of the dryer (or off the line when I hung things up), and dump it all in a basket. Then I'd start the cycle again, which meant we ended up with pawed-through piles of clean clothes on the laundry-room floor after people found the clean stuff they needed to wear, and they never bothered to put their clean clothes away. I was just as guilty as everyone else in just not wanting to put away my laundry. But with the clean laundry growing like fungus on the laundry room floor, it's no wonder we couldn't keep the laundry room neat.

Then inspiration hit me one day in the shower, when I was reading "lather, rinse, repeat" on my shampoo bottle. Then I thought, "wash, dry, put away, repeat." Why not make that my new laundry mantra?

So I did. And here's why it works: There's an implied rule that goes along with this saying. You can't get from "wash" to "repeat" until you finish the two steps in between. So now, instead of doing back-to-back, marathon loads of laundry, I play a little mental game with myself. I have to wash, dry, and then put away the previous load before I allow myself to start a new load of laundry. So far it's been working great for keeping our laundry room clutter free. Why not give it a try in your house?

DO YOU HAVE TOO MANY CLOTHES, LINENS, AND TOWELS TO BEGIN WITH?

There is one behavior that I was guilty of when I was living in a cluttered house. I've mentioned this before: If I couldn't find something that I needed, I usually ended up going out and buying it a second time. The same held true for clothing we needed but hadn't gotten around to washing or couldn't find.

During our spendthrift days, it didn't faze us to go out and buy new underwear or socks when we couldn't find clean ones, or a shirt the kids needed to wear for a school play when we were unable to locate the shirt that we knew we owned. There were even times when we were having house guests and I ended up buying a new sheet set just so we could have clean sheets for the guest room bed.

Nonetheless, this panicked shopping resulted in our having too many of nearly everything that ends up in the laundry room. Do you really need two week's worth of underwear (fourteen pair) or a month's worth of socks (thirty pair) or twelve sets of twin sheets when there are only four twin beds in the house? At most I should have had eight sets of these sheets so that one set is always clean for my girls' bedrooms (a twin bed each) and the guest room (two twin beds). Then again once I started following my own "wash, dry, put away, repeat" mantra, I should never be without clean sheets again should company show up.

TOO MUCH LAUNDRY TO WASH

So let's say that you do, in fact, come to the realization that you have too many things that need to be laundered. How do you cut down on your stash without wasting your money?

1. Turn some of the nonessential but worn-out pieces of clothing and linens into rags for free cleaning tools. This will help save you money in the future so you don't need to buy paper towels.

2. Donate towels, sheets, and blankets that you no longer want to keep on heavy rotation. If they are worn out, you can bring these to a local animal shelter. They use them in pens and after surgery and baths. If these linens are still half decent, I'll bet a Goodwill location or other thrift store that supports a good cause will take these off your hands for you. Best of all, you will likely get a tax receipt for your in-kind donation, which would be like getting cash back for your good deed.

Getting Your Garage Under Control

Do you live in a home with a two-car garage that you never use for parked cars? If so, been there, done that. And hated every minute of it. Why oh why was it so impossible to keep a garage neat enough so that I could use it for its actual purpose—holding cars? Well, there was a method to my clutter madness and maybe yours, too. For starters, even though we didn't *park* the cars in the garage, we *entered* the house through the door in the garage. How many times have you come home from grocery shopping, so exhausted you could barely see, and the task of putting away the groceries was too daunting to deal with? So you didn't, and you put your groceries on the garage floor, just for a minute, but that's where they stayed, in your makeshift, horizontal pantry, until you actually needed those groceries? Yup, guilty as charged.

Then there was the issue of the garage becoming a catchall space for all of our outdoor-related things that you might store in a shed but don't—because you haven't organized your shed and have no room or, like our old house, you just didn't have a shed at all. Think sports equipment, extra food, gardening tools, the lawn mower, shovels, and more. Some of this stuff definitely belongs in here, because it makes sense. Need to shovel the driveway? It's convenient having the shovels right there when you leave the garage on a snowy day. Want to mow the lawn? Just roll the lawn mower out of the garage and get started cutting the grass in the front yard. Sounds reasonable, right?

Finally, in our old neighborhood there was an ordinance that you were not allowed to store your garbage cans outside, where people on the street could see them. This meant that along with all the other things I mentioned we stored in our garage, we had

If your garage looks like this, you may think you'll never be able to use it to park your car—but you'll get there, if you remove what you don't need and organize what you do.

to stash our mammoth, trash-company-provided, rolling trash cart along with our recycle bins in our garage.

As you can imagine this meant that our garage was just busting at the seams with stuff. And the worst part? Because there was no rhyme or reason to where or how we stored everything, we were always losing things. It's frustrating to know that I own eight pairs of gardening gloves, three pairs of hedge clippers and two rakes, all because when I needed the gloves or the clippers, or a rake—and couldn't find one of them in the garage—I went out to the store and bought another. With all this stuff it's no wonder we never got a car in the garage.

So how do you get back control of your garage and avoid spending unnecessary money the way I did? Here are some organizing methods to try.

ARRANGE BY CATEGORY

A great way to get your organizing started is to begin grouping items by category. Think about what you have in your garage and how you can put like things together. Put everything for gardening and lawn care in one spot and all your trash and recycling containers in another. Kids' bikes and sporting equipment should be clustered somewhere else. Remember, you're just sorting stuff for now, not finding a permanent home for it—that comes a wee bit later.

Depending on how much stuff you have, you may have to wait until a day when the weather cooperates so that you can spread out onto the driveway (and lawn and sidewalk, if needed). Again, this is just a temporary way of figuring exactly what you've been stashing in your garage all this time.

What's It Worth?

When we were clearing out our garage and basement, we came across some very old tools that my father-in-law had acquired from his father, and that my husband acquired from him. Some of these things looked like torture devices—one is a clamp that's as big as a tennis racket and as thick as a Louisville Slugger—and while my husband is still holding on to them, because he might need them one day, the truth is they may have some value beyond his workshop.

"Like with anything that is older, old tools can be considered to be antiques," says Jeff Jeffers, CEO and principal auctioneer at Garth Auctioneers. Jeffers says that when it comes to an old tool, it's good if you can figure out its "circa" date—might be right on the tool itself—and where in America or elsewhere in the world the tool originated. For example, Jeffers says that the Pennsylvania Dutch are known to be great ironsmiths, so tools coming from there—especially if they depict hearts, pinwheels, and tulips—will have more value, albeit from an artistic, decorative point of view. "Great ironwork and metalwork can be considered folk art," adds Jeffers, and these will be of interest to people who collect these kinds of things or like to decorate their homes with them.

REVIEW WHAT YOU OWN AND WHAT YOU DON'T NEED

Now that you've got your garage stuff grouped together, take some time to really look through what you've found. Do you have

Quick Clutter Challenge

Does your supermarket give you cash off your grocery bill if you bring your own bags with you to the checkout counter? Where I live, that discount ranges from two to five cents per bag. Even Target gives you five cents per bag for bringing your own. Hey, if you fill ten bags of groceries, that's twenty to fifty cents you've saved—just as good as any coupon you might have cut out of your Sunday newspaper.

So focus on stashed bags for this Quick Clutter Challenge. Set your timer for fifteen minutes, and see how many bags you can find that you can take with you to the grocery store the next time to shop. It doesn't matter if they're plastic bags, brown sacks, or reusable canvas bags that you got specifically for carrying your groceries: just any bag that you can take to the store and carry home full.

Once you have found these bags, find a tidy and easy-to-remember place for them. I like to stash these bags in my trunk, so they're always on hand when I go to the store. You may find it easier to have them somewhere inside the house. The bottom line: You have to bring them with you to save money on your groceries, so don't hide them on yourself. Ready, set, go find those bags!

multiple pairs of gardening gloves, hedge trimmers, and rakes like I do? Do you need them all? If not, are any so worn out that they should hit the trash? Or are the ones you don't think you need still good enough that you can sell them for cash?

Also, if you've been keeping anything, in hopes you might need it someday, well, today is that someday. For example: Because we have a dog and I don't want to buy "poop" bags to clean up after him, I hoard plastic bags—anything from ones you get at the grocery store, to bags the bread comes in, to the plastic sleeve that holds our daily newspaper. When I finally went through our belongings in the garage, I found more plastic bags than I could have ever used, even if I had *four* dogs, let alone one. Since plastic bags don't have much value on the free market, I divided my stash in half, and took the remaining bags to the plastic bag recycle bin at my local supermarket. At least this way, in addition to clearing out my plastic bag clutter, I also contributed to turning these plastic bags into something useful.

This exercise in reviewing what you have in your garage is also an opportunity to determine if you've been storing things that no longer fit your current lifestyle. I had a good chuckle one day when we sifted through our garage stuff and found a pair of Barbie roller skates and a tiny kid's bicycle—things my daughters hadn't used for at least five years. What the heck were we thinking, holding on to them for so long? Truth is, we *forgot* we even owned them because they'd gotten lost in all the clutter. (We ended up selling them on Craigslist for some quick cash.)

SET UP DESIGNATED SPACES
IN THE GARAGE

Now is your chance to start putting things back in an orderly fashion. You should store groups of items in spaces that make the most sense based on how you use them. Those aforementioned poop bags that I'd hoarded? I stashed the thinned collection in a giant plastic bag, and hung it from the wall, next to the dog's leash, near the garage entrance into the house. The kids' sports equipment and bikes—the ones that actually fit them and that they could use? We etched out a spot in the front corner of the garage since the kids were most likely to want to pull out their scooter or grab their helmet, and get right out onto the driveway.

We did end up investing in an oversized Rubbermaid container to hold the kids' odds and ends—bicycle pump, wrist guards for roller skating, jump ropes—rather than hanging them up on the wall with hooks. This is because, frankly, my kids are better about cleaning up after themselves if they can dump their stuff when they were done with it, rather than hanging stuff back up on the wall. This also saved me from having to nag them constantly and made for a much more peaceful give-and-take in the garage—and a neater space in the end.

We couldn't decide the best place for the trash cans, to be honest with you. Part of me wanted them right by the entrance into the house so I didn't have to walk too far to throw something out or to separate my recyclables. Then there was another part of me that wanted them near the front of the garage to keep the smell of rotting garbage as far away as possible from the entrance to the house. This positioning also meant I would spend less time putting out the trash, because the cans were closest to the front of the garage anyway. So the garbage cans ended up as drifters in the garage, based on how close to trash day we were. But with the rest of the garage organized and neat, this one tiny snafu in our plan didn't end up being a huge deal overall.

Remember, you've got to create spaces for these like things in a way that works for *you*, not based on what worked for *me*.

TAKE ADVANTAGE OF ALL USABLE SPACE

Of course it makes sense to store the things that need to be in the garage on the perimeter of the garage. But don't forget that there is other usable space that you can take advantage of here.

O If your garage is unfinished, you can tuck things like skis and shovels in between the studs.

O Install shelves in the garage so you can do more than just stack stuff on the floor. When we redid our kitchen, we took the old kitchen cabinets and reinstalled them in the garage for extra storage so my husband could have a workspace. It's also where we ended up keeping all of his tools.

O Hang up whatever you can to make even more room on the floor. I've seen garages with all kinds of things hanging from the walls and the rafters. You can invest in durable hooks to hold bikes, and even some nails hammered into a wall stud can hold up things like jump ropes, folding chairs for sideline watching at sporting events—especially if they come in their own carrying case—and reusable shopping bags. In our old house my husband rigged an elaborate pulley system to hold tarps that he didn't want to leave folded up on the floor, where mice might like to set up their little homes! But you could do something similar with light things you wanted to get off the floor, like skis or overflow duffel bags.

PUT EVERYTHING BACK WHERE IT BELONGS WHEN YOU'RE DONE WITH IT

This probably sounds like broken-record advice—this notion of putting things back where they belong, once you're done using them—but it really is the cornerstone of a neat and orderly house. Also, once you've got order and storage solutions in your garage that make sense for your needs, it should be much easier for everyone in your family to clean up after themselves—because they know where everything goes. And if you have to end up creating a dumping container of kid's outdoor toys like I did—because it saves your sanity—that's okay, too. At least you'll always know where their stuff is and your garage won't look like a toy store after Black Friday sales!

Bearing Down on the Basement

Like the garage, it's easy for a basement to become a catchall area of your home. It's the place where you may be storing your kids' toys and clothes, old tools, and anything else that you couldn't figure out where to put in your house—so you put it in the basement.

The good news is getting your basement in order is a lot like getting your garage in order. So if you've already tackled that project, you're in good shape. If not, here's a quick recap of how you can apply the same organizational approach to your basement that you used in your garage.

Think your basement can never look like this one? Think again!

CLEAR OUT THE JUNK FIRST

Because a basement is heated, you are likely to store more delicate items there. This could be old paint cans or overflow clothing. Before you can get the basement organized, you need to get rid of everything that's taking up extra space and which you really don't need anymore.

For example, it's smart to store the paint that you use on the walls of your house in the basement. That's because you don't want paint to be exposed to extreme temperatures, which will shorten the usable life of the paint. But if it's been more than ten years since you bought a new can of paint—and you never opened it—or as long as five years since you touched an opened can of

Paint Swap

Ever bought too much paint for a project—or have a few gallons left over from that project you just never started? As you know paint isn't cheap—about $25 for a gallon—but this money and those cans of paint don't have to go to waste!

Organize a paint swap with some friends who may be interested in repainting a room but, like you, don't want to spend money on new paint they may not end up using. Ask your friends to each bring over two to four cans of paint they are willing to part with and that aren't too old to use. Together you might be able to find new colors to brighten up your walls without spending a dime. Walking away with two gallons of latex paint will save you $50!

paint, it's time to get rid of it. (Yes, even paint has an expiration date.) Wait to discard this paint at one of your area's "household hazardous waste" collection days. This way you know that someone will safely discard the paint. Never pour it down the drain!

If you store off-season clothes, extra toys, and holiday decorations in the basement, now would be a good time to go through all of them and see how you might thin your collection. Start by creating three piles: toss, keep, and sell. Then once you're done figuring out which of the piles each item belongs in, you can start cleaning up and neatening up your basement space.

Waterproof Bins

Always store everything in your basement in waterproof bins or on shelving at least a foot off the floor. Not everyone's basement floods, but the risk of unexpected leaks and storms is high enough that it will pay to be cautious. Plus, if you don't have a dehumidifier running 24/7 in your basement, you're already dealing with a perpetually damp space. Waterproof bins—complete with well-fitting tops—help ward off mold and mildew year round and make it possible to create some elbow room in your drawers and closets.

Clearly you don't need to put paint cans and the like in a waterproof bin, but if you can keep anything made of metal elevated off the floor, you'll save yourself some trouble if water does find its way into your basement. You don't need any rust to go with your house paint.

A PLACE FOR EVERYTHING

Just as you did in the garage, you need to create specific spaces in your basement for everything that you have downstairs. Even without a finished basement you can identify certain areas where you can group like things together. One corner can be where you keep all the painting supplies—cans of paint, brushes, rollers, and drop cloths—and along another wall you can stack bins of your off-season clothes.

Unlike other parts of the house, a basement presents certain challenges when it comes to hanging things up because its walls are likely either poured concrete or cinder block. This means that you can't exactly hammer a nail into that kind of wall. So when getting your basement organized and decluttered, it would be a good idea to find shelving units from elsewhere in the house that you no longer need that you can reuse in the basement to store things on. Or maybe you can look for free shelves someone is giving away on Freecycle or Craigslist. Whatever you do, don't put off neatening your basement because you don't have shelves to use. Figure out a Plan B—even if it's just stacking clearly labeled storage bins, one on top of the other—as your way of getting your basement neat and orderly.

Attacking Clutter in the Attic

Recently, I was watching the show *Clean House*, and the program was highlighting some of the messiest homes in America. One of these houses was piled so high with clutter that it had spilled out into the garage and up into the attic. In fact, it was so bad that when you pulled down the stairs into the attic, all you could do was climb to the top and look around. There wasn't an inch of space for a person to walk up there. Even worse, the weight of all of that clutter had actually cracked the ceiling of the living room below.

I feel thankful that my clutter problem never got that bad, but that's not to say that my attic didn't, at one point, have things I was holding onto for reasons I couldn't explain. I know that a big part of our problem in the attic had to do with how we moved into this house. It was a frenzied day when we took ownership, and with only a small basement and no garage, the things we didn't know what to do with ended up in the attic. We didn't put a lot up there, but once I decided to take back control of the attic space, I found things that left me wondering, "What was I thinking?"

I know that I'm guilty of the "someday I might need that" mentality, but looking at some of the things I unearthed from the attic, I know I could have saved myself lots of trouble if I'd made some not-so-tough decisions before the clutter had taken root. Why had I not simply thrown them out or sold things I knew I wouldn't need in the first place? Ah, the million-dollar question and the crux of our collective clutter problem.

OUT OF SIGHT, OUT OF MIND

One of the challenges of using a space like the attic to store things is the "out of sight, out of mind" mentality that you can fall into, an unfortunate state of mind I've mentioned before. (Are you picking up on a trend here?) You forget about the clutter you've been hanging onto because you don't have to see it on a daily basis.

Thankfully, this is no longer the situation in our attic. Currently, we store only seasonal decorations in the attic. That means that whenever I go up into the attic, I never face the surprise of finding something that I should have tossed out long ago; but that wasn't always the case.

Before wrestling back control of the attic, we had a variety of items stored up there that we had quickly stashed there on moving-in day. It was the best idea for getting them out of the way for the time being, but then we promptly forgot that we'd stored those things up there, and before we knew it, three years had gone by.

How Long to Hold Onto Stuff

Remember the hanger trick from Chapter 6 that you can use to thin out your wardrobe seasonally? You should take a similar approach with other "someday" stuff that you keep on hand. For example, if you have been holding onto packets of seeds because you wanted to grow a garden, make this year the year you decide if you're actually going to use your green thumb. Then, if planting season comes and goes and you never got around to starting those seeds, accept your reality and get rid of them! They may not take up much space, but they can be small indicators of a larger clutter problem. Start thinking about your clutter in terms of expiration dates, and if months and years have come and gone, it's time to toss that stuff.

One of these items was a full-sized bed frame that we'd brought with us from our old house. Before we moved, I did all the right things by trying to sell it on Craigslist (no luck), then giving it away on Freecycle (no luck again). I should have just put it out with the trash on moving day, but my husband insisted we keep it. It's a solid cherry headboard/footboard combination with a bed frame, and it was always our plan to use it in our guest room.

But somewhere along the way two things happened. First, in one of our many moves, we cracked the headboard. Then, we upgraded our own bed from a full to a queen to a king, tossed the mattresses we'd used before, and no longer had a full-sized mattress to use with the frame. My husband swore he would fix the headboard so we could reuse it, but once it was in the guest room, we'd need to spend money on a new full-sized mattress, not to mention new sheets and blankets to fit the bed since we no longer owned any. We could try to sell it again, but since he never fixed it, I knew no one would want it. So up into the attic it went, where we promptly forgot about it.

Enter the days of decluttering, and I found myself wondering why on earth we still had that darned bed frame. It had been sitting untouched for years in the attic, and we had made no effort to get rid of it. But since we'd determined that our attic would be used primarily for seasonal decorations—as a way of keeping what was up there neat and organized—the bed frame had to get out of the attic. Finally, I put my foot down and declared that if we weren't going to reuse it as our guest room bed—which meant purchasing the aforementioned bedding supplies—it was time to bid adieu to that piece of furniture. So we did.

What's the moral of this section in regards to your attic? Please try not to fall into the "out of sight, out of mind" mentality by doing what we used to do and just stashing things in your attic thinking that you might need them one day. I believe in the notion of holding onto something useful, but you should do so in a way that you can quickly locate that "I may need it someday" item, rather than having to drag down the attic ladder and paw through a bunch of dusty stuff in hopes that you'll uncover the item. In retrospect, if we had been serious about reusing that headboard and footboard in our guest bedroom, we should have stored it right in the guest bedroom. This would have provided us with a regular reminder to put the bed frame together and use it for our guests or to put it out with the trash once and for all.

DEFINE HOW YOU USE THE ATTIC

I believe that our decision to use our attic solely for seasonal decorations has helped us to keep that space clutter-free because it has a well-defined purpose. Before we made this designation, you might have found Christmas wrapping paper in the basement, Thanksgiving decorations stashed in the kitchen, and Easter eggs still scattered around the playroom, even though we were well into summer. Now, when we move on from one season or holiday to another, our plan is simple and organized.

1. We take down the Rubbermaid containers that we use to store the just-passed holiday's decorations in. If there are leftover decorations in the container that we didn't get around to using, we seriously consider

whether or not we'll likely use them again in the future. If not, we put them aside to sell or give away.

2. As we're putting away the decorations, we evaluate their condition. If something broke during that decorating season, we determine if we can fix it right away—before the rest of that holiday's decorations are stored back up in the attic. If we can't fix it or aren't interested in fixing it, we'll throw it right away. No sense in packing up a broken decoration.

3. We put those containers back up in the attic.

4. Next, we take down the similar Rubbermaid containers that contain the upcoming holiday's decorations, and begin our decorating task. Again, as we're pulling stuff out, we evaluate its condition to see if anything broke in transit or has somehow fallen out of favor. If it's still in good condition but we're no longer interested in keeping it, we'll put it aside to sell. If it's as good as junk, we throw it out.

5. As soon as we're finished decorating for the current holiday, we put those containers back up into the attic. Because if we don't take care of them right away, the containers themselves would soon become clutter and who knows? We might mistakenly try to store something else in them, leaving us in a lurch when, a few weeks later, we need to clean up from the current holiday and don't have the expected empty container available for storage.

One last trick we use: When we're putting everything back into the attic, we move the storage bin to the very back of the attic and shift the containers in front of it forward. This makes it easier for us to find the next holiday's decoration container because it's closer to the front of the attic.

Cashing In
Jason, California

I participate in a lot of triathlons and other road races, and when you go to these events, you get stuff from the sponsors. I've gotten new shoes and bikes for free, from winning drawings, and if they don't end up working out for my needs, I would toss them in the garage. Or, when I get a new bike, I might change out certain things about it and end up with extra equipment. For example, I have a bike that I've been racing on for a while now but the stem is too long. So I bought a shorter stem, and then I ended up with an extra stem. I've had this happen with extra bike wheels, too. Sometimes I buy stuff for my bike and it doesn't work out, and that ends up in the garage, too.

Eventually, I decided I didn't want this clutter in my garage anymore, and I started selling the equipment on eBay. For example, once I bought a carbon fiber wheel set for my bike for $199 on eBay, but they were mislabeled and didn't work on my bike. I know that those wheels normally sell for something like $1,300 so I turned around and relisted them on eBay; I got $250 for them. And when things I buy don't work out, like those wheels, I'll just sell them right back to someone else on eBay and make my money back. So I've made money and I've cleared out the sports equipment clutter from my garage.

TOSS	KEEP	SELL
Cans of unopened paint older than ten years or opened paint that you've had for five years or more, particularly any that don't match your current wall colors	Paint for touch ups on walls in your house	Unwanted, newer paint (or swap with friends, or recycle during a local "household hazardous waste" day)
Outdoor toys and sports equipment that is broken, missing parts, or has been recalled via the Consumer Products Safety Commission (*www.cpsc.gov*)	Bikes, sporting equipment, and other playthings that your kids still use on a regular basis	Bikes, sporting equipment, and play stuff that your kids have outgrown or are no longer interested in playing with
Broken furniture you've been storing for someday	Furniture that you can figure out how to use now	Furniture that's still in good shape and might be worth something on Craigslist
Broken or worn-out holiday decorations	Decorations with sentimental value or which you plan to use the next holiday season	Decorations still in good condition but which you don't want to keep anymore
Worn-out linens that aren't worthy of becoming rags	Linens and towels in good condition	Donate older linens to a good cause

Total Cash Back in This Chapter

When thinking about the rooms and areas of the home we tackled in this chapter, we often think of them as "out of sight, out of mind." These are the places where we tend to toss and hide a lot of clutter, and I'm hoping that at this point, not only have you cleared out that clutter, but you've also made some money from it.

Perhaps you've figured out that, based on the amount of laundry you're always doing, you have too many clothes—so you've thinned your wardrobe and have perhaps consigned some of it to a resale shop. Or you've gone through your kids' outdoor toys and figured out which ones you could sell for a profit—I got $20 for a Cozy Coupe car my kids could no longer fit in. (I think I bought it used from a neighbor for about the same amount!) Maybe you've decided to take a page from my attic organization, and dedicate that space to seasonal decorations only—and were able to sell some holiday knick-knacks to bring in extra cash. You also know just how valuable old tools and sporting goods can be when you know what to sell and who wants to buy them!

Finally, I helped you to figure out how best to use your basement space. You now know what to do with any house paint you may have been storing down there and how you could swap paint you no longer need with friends and neighbors to save some bucks in the long run. You also know how to protect even moisture-sensitive items in your basement by using a combination of shelving and waterproof storage that will keep the room tidy and your belongings safe from water damage and mildew.

Total Cash Back in This Chapter: **$300**

chapter 8

PUTTING ORDER BACK IN YOUR CLOSETS, PANTRY, AND MUDROOM

You'll have a real sense that you've tackled your clutter problem when you can open any of the closets in your home or walk into the pantry, and you don't have to duck in fear of what might come tumbling down on top of you. Or you can enter your house through the mudroom and walk from the door to the end of the room without having to step over or weave your way around something on the floor. It takes time to get these areas of the home in this state, but using my step-by-step approach, you can accomplish this with a little persistence.

The Key to Organized Closets

In Chapter 6, Making Sense of the Master and Other Bedrooms, I touched on the topic of how to organize everyday clothing in your bedroom closets. In this section of the book I'll revisit the clothing conundrum in the closet, albeit briefly, and I'll also delve a bit deeper into how you can use your closets—no matter what they hold—in an optimal way. We're talking about shoes, linens, off-season clothing, and more.

STORING EVERYDAY CLOTHING

If you have trouble finding your everyday clothing or figuring out what to wear with what, why not hang your clothes up in a way that makes this easier on you? For example, my husband's side of the closet is divided into three distinct areas. In these areas he hangs the following:

○ work pants

○ work and button-down shirts

○ blazers and suit jackets

When he gets dressed in the morning, it's easy for him to pick one piece from each of these sections and to get out the door in no time. Additionally, when it's time to put away laundry, it's a no brainer because he can see exactly where all his clothes belong.

If you have little kids, you can try a similar system or maybe you want to match up outfits and hang them up together. This way as your kids get older and want to dress themselves, they can take down a prefab outfit from their closet and get dressed without much fuss.

There's another benefit to matching up outfits like this—whether you're doing it for your kids or clustering clothes that look good together in your own closet: It forces you to review each piece of clothing and really consider what it goes with or how much you want to work it into your wardrobe. Then, if you find yourself holding a shirt, pair of pants, or skirt—and you're really conflicted about where it belongs—that could be a hint that it's time to let go of that article of clothing.

SHOES IN THE CLOSET

I remember from the cable TV series *Sex and the City* how the character Carrie Bradshaw had all of her shoes stacked in their original boxes, with a picture on the front of the shoes inside. It looked very good on camera and was perfect for her fashionista ways, but in reality I don't know how practical that kind of shoe storage would be for me. I don't have that kind of love-affair relationship with my shoes—meaning I don't spend hundreds and hundreds of dollars on them and then need to protect them like museum pieces. At the same time I want easy access to my shoes so getting dressed in the morning is easier for me.

First, though, you need to ensure that all the shoes in your closet—or the shoes in each of your family member's closets—are those that they regularly wear. If not, put them aside to toss or sell. Now let's focus our attention on the remainders.

As far as how *you* should store your shoes in a way that is neat and practical, you need to find a system that works for your lifestyle and the space where you'll be storing your shoes. We have built-in, skinny shelves in our closet where I can slip my shoes at the end of the day. Each of my daughters has a similar setup, but they don't bother to neatly put away their shoes, and my life is too short to fight with them about that. So we've put baskets in their closets so that at least when they kick off their shoes, they're landing (hopefully) in a single container. Maybe those over-the-door shoe holders would work well if you have limited floor space and you know you would be disciplined about putting away your shoes in pairs at the end of the day. Basically, you need to neaten up how you store your shoes and to choose a system that works for your way of life, just as the baskets work for my kids.

 **Cashing In**
Jennifer, New York

At one point I had a huge Christmas list: Thanks to a large family and a huge social network, I was exchanging gifts with about fifty people a year. That meant that in any given year, I might end up with close to one hundred gifts in the years that people were feeling generous. While my friends and family were usually spot-on with their gift selections, many times I got gifts that were just not for me. Since I couldn't return them (no receipt, no evidence of what store they came from, or I was just too darn lazy to do it), I ended up stuffing them into the bottom of my closet and forgetting about them.

But about seven years ago, I was inspired to do something about the clutter. My cousins sold their old Cabbage Patch Kids and HeMan toys on eBay and were making really good money for them. I began to look around my home to see if I had anything of value, and off I went selling stuff. Getting two iPods for Christmas one year really pushed me to try my hand at making money selling things online. While some people could just take an iPod back to an Apple store, I didn't live anywhere near one. So I decided to take the iPod I didn't need and list it on eBay. I ended up getting $400 for it! Over time I've sold a number of items from my home—both gifts and other clutter. Even a pair of worn-out Prada shoes found a home and got me $40 in the process.

But where I really hit pay dirt was when I realized I had five different pieces of Tiffany jewelry and accessories that were just taking up space in my jewelry box. After researching how much Tiffany items typically went for on eBay, I listed the five pieces—a keychain, two bracelets, a piggy bank, and a ring—in separate auctions, and waited for the bids to start rolling in. By the time all five auctions had ended, I'd gotten $1,000 for those five pieces.

My advice for selling valuable items on eBay? Write an eye-catching headline ("Authentic Tiffany Keychain"), and a friendly, detailed description of your product. Even though eBayers tend to be snobby, they want to do business with someone they like. So the friendlier you sound, the more likely people are to bid on your item. Also, be sure to do an Advanced Search on eBay for similar items that have already sold. You can see not only how much they went for, but what category they sold in and at what price the seller started the bidding. All the information you need to assess the value of your item is right there on eBay.

OFF-SEASON CLOTHING

Not everyone is fortunate enough to have a gigantic closet in the bedroom in which to store off-season clothing. When my kids were little, I would put their opposite season clothing in file boxes, and store them on a shelf. These days I'm using the dresser in the guest bedroom as an off-season clothing closet. But here are two ways that you can logically store off-season clothing in a closet.

First, you can dedicate one closet in the house for just that purpose. Maybe now that you've minimized your laundry, towels, and linens, you've opened up a closet. That could be the space you use. Or maybe you can make a closet in the basement with a hanging rack and a set of shelves for the off-season clothes.

The second idea will make good use of your luggage. I'll bet you've got a couple of suitcases lying around the house somewhere. Are you storing them in a haphazard place? Why not put them to good use, and pack away your off-season clothing in those suitcases? If you don't have room in a closet to fit these suitcases, you can always slide them under the bed.

BED SHEETS, PILLOWS, AND BLANKETS

In the previous chapter on dealing with laundry, I offered some advice for figuring out the quantity of bed linens you should have so that you don't overwhelm yourself. Here's how those numbers add up, when looking at them per bed (not bedroom), in the house:

O   One to two sheet sets

O   One to two blankets, unless you keep your home chilly like we do. Then keeping three blankets per bed would be a good idea—that is, blankets that you could easily layer if you got chilly at night. For example, on my bed in the winter, we have a down comforter, a cotton blanket, and a duvet to top it off. In the summer, we have just the comforter and cotton blanket.

O Two pillows per person per bed

A few years ago I picked up a great trick for storing bed sheets. I fold them up and stick them inside the pillowcase that matches the set. For sets with more than one pillowcase, I put the second or any subsequent pillowcases inside as well. This way when it comes time to make a bed, I just have to grab the pillowcase sack filled with sheets, and I'm good to go. In your linen closet you can make your life even easier by storing these sacks by size bed they fit—twin, full, queen, and king. Put the blankets and pillows that match these sizes on these shelves, too.

Here's another reason I like this pillowcase storage option: Once I decided to match all the sheets up like this, I quickly realized which sheets I was still stuffing inside my linen closet that no longer belonged to a set. This made thinning my linens super easy: If a sheet was solo now, I put it in the basement with my painting supplies so I could reuse it as a drop cloth, or I put it in my "to donate" pile so I could bring it to my local animal shelter. Or if the sheets were in good enough condition, albeit without their matching counterparts, I could consider selling them at my next yard sale.

TOWELS FOR ALL OCCASIONS

Just as you might decide to divide how you store bed sheets based on size, you can take this approach with your towels, too. Personally, I like to store towels near the bathrooms where I use them, or in the case of our pool towels, in the coat closet on the way out to the pool. But if you have a dedicated linen closet where it makes the most sense to store all of your linens—towels, sheets, and more—then you have a different task. You need to make sure that each and every towel that you fold up and put away in that closet is in perfect condition. Also, you need to figure out if you actually have *too many* towels. If so, it's time to thin the crop.

At a minimum you should have two towels per person in your home, plus two towels per guest you can accommodate in your home. These are bath towels. You can use a similar formula for figuring out how many pool towels to keep on hand during the summer months. As far as hand towels for the bathrooms, two per bathroom that you rotate is a good number. And what about reusable towels that you might be using in the kitchen as a replacement for paper towels? A week's worth—or seven—would be a good place to start. You can always recycle/reuse older hand towels from the bathroom as the towels you use in the kitchen.

THE COAT CLOSET

There's no rule that says that you have to hang things or store them in a traditional fashion in your coat closet. For example, if you happen to own any horizontal hanging organizers designed to hold sweaters in a closet, you can use them to hold hats, gloves, mittens, and scarves in the winter, and then beach towels, pool toys, and sun-block in the summer.

No matter what you choose to store in your coat closet—even if it's just coats—the trick to getting that to be an organized space, one you'll have an easy time keeping neat, is making sure it has a defined purpose and everyone in the family knows it. Even if you have to go as far as labeling the bins you use or the dividers you hang in the closet, at least everything is there in black and white to explain exactly how people are supposed to use that closet.

Quick Clutter Challenge

If you've ever bought a bedroom set, then you know that these sets often come with multiple items, not all of which you end up using in your bedroom. I know that in our house, our beds are not really set up to take bed skirts—a bed skirt on a daybed just doesn't work—so I've got at least three never-used bed skirts sitting in my linen closet. I'm guessing that there's someone out there who likes bed skirts and has the bedroom furniture for them, and that person might just want to buy these bed skirts from me.

Do you have similar items in your linen closet—sitting around unused and taking up space? For this chapter's Quick Clutter Challenge, I want you to find all of these things—whether they are bed skirts or sleeping bags your kids no longer use—so you can sell them for cash. Set your timer for fifteen minutes and ready, set, go find some linens you can list on Craigslist or sell at a yard sale!

Tips for Getting Your Pantry in Tip-Top Shape

If you're lucky enough to have a pantry closet, then you know how easy it is to overload it with supplies. Having this extra storage space seems to encourage one to stock up—perhaps overstock—the shelves, and without an organizational system in place, in no time it might look like a bomb went off in your pantry. Consider these tips for getting your pantry in tip-top shape. Keep in mind that, even if you don't have a pantry, these tips would apply to any of your kitchen cabinets where you're stocking food.

GROUP LIKE THINGS TOGETHER IN THE PANTRY

Perhaps you're already grouping all the canned goods on one shelf and the boxed snacks on another. Take that grouping one level deeper: Put all the canned *vegetables* together, and then within the vegetable group, put corn with corn, beans with beans, etc. The same goes for chips, pretzels, and cake mixes.

MAKE IT EASIER FOR PEOPLE TO GET SNACKS

Whenever you buy a box of individually wrapped snacks, tear the top off the box. This way when people want a granola bar or snack-sized bag of crackers, all they need to do is reach into the box, rather than pull down the box, open it up, take out what they need, and potentially not put the box back where it belongs.

CREATE A SNACK BASKET

If you're doling out single servings of snacks—whether those you buy prepackaged or by making your own with baggies you buy and fill—keep all of them in a pretty wicker basket on a shelf low enough so little hands can reach them. By using one basket, you let your kids know where they can grab a snack without making a mess and you'll know when you're running low on snacks with just a quick glance at how full the basket is.

TAKE ADVANTAGE OF YOUR PANTRY DOOR

An over-the-door shoe organizer is a great tool to use in the pantry—especially if you have the kind with see-through pockets. These pockets are the perfect size for storing those smaller pantry items that easily tip over or could get lost. These are things such as boxes of pudding and Jell-O mix, food coloring, and spices.

SET UP TRAYS TO HOLD MESSY ITEMS

No matter how well I wipe down the bottle of olive oil or soy sauce, I always seem to leave a bit of residue on the bottom of the bottle—which leaves a ring on my pantry shelf. A great way to neaten your pantry and keep messes at bay is to find serving trays you no longer use and reuse them as shelf liners. You can group your messy ingredients together on these trays—oils, vinegars, and sauces on one, and flour and sugar on another. When your things get a little grimy, you can take the whole tray to the sink and wipe it down.

FOOD STORAGE DEADLINES: NONPERISHABLES

FOOD	SHELF LIFE OF NONPERISHABLES
Pasta sauce or salsa in a jar	Up to a year
Dried spices	One to three years (If you pinch the spice and can't tell its original aroma, it's time to replace it.)
Baking mixes (cakes, cookies, pancakes, muffins, etc.)	Follow the "best used by" date
Breakfast cereal	Six to twelve months (unopened) or "best used by date"; two to three months if opened
Cooking oils	Twelve to twenty-four months
Canned fruits and vegetables	"Best used by" date or about three years (Note: Any canned food that has a bulge or hisses when you open it is contaminated and should be tossed in the trash, regardless of how recently you purchased it.)
Condiments (ketchup, mayonnaise, mustard)	As long as twenty-four months or the "best used by" date
Canned or bottled juice	Twelve to eighteen months (Keep in mind that the longer you store juice, the less potent the vitamin C concentration will be.)

STORE ODD-SIZED THINGS IN UNIFORM-SIZED CONTAINERS

Anything in your pantry that comes in a box, bag, or package that isn't easily stackable will be hard to keep organized. It would be better to transfer those products from their original, odd-sized packages to something that's more uniform. This could be Mason jars or glass pasta sauce jars that you've rinsed out and can use to hold things like chocolate chips, oatmeal, or flour. Or you could use clear plastic containers or even the shoeboxes I mentioned in Chapter 1, Organization Tools You Probably Already Own. The idea here isn't to make more work for yourself by transferring things, but rather making it easier in the long run to keep your pantry shelves neat and tidy by utilizing containers that stack easily.

MAKE A MAKE-A-MEAL BIN

If you know you're going to have some busy nights during the week, why not dedicate a bin or a basket in your pantry to make-a-meal ingredients? This is where you can toss everything you'll need to get dinner on the table, save for anything perishable that might be in the refrigerator. Then whenever it's time to cook, you don't have to go rooting through the pantry, pulling all your ingredients together. Instead, you can just grab the bin or basket off the shelf, take whatever you need from the fridge, and you can get cooking.

175

Turn a Messy Mudroom into a Space You Can Use

When we decided to take back control of our mudroom, we needed to figure out first exactly how we used this space in our house—or wanted to use it. And this was it: We wanted it to be the "ground zero," if you will, for our kids when they come home from school. We wanted it to be the place where they could hang up their coats, put their backpacks, and kick off their shoes. Only problem? In its current state we didn't have anything in the space that would actually allow the kids to do that. Up until this point the mudroom was the dumping room, with everyone quite literally just dumping everything on the floor when they came in the door.

To achieve our goal we did the following three things:

1. Put up pegboards with enough pegs to allow everyone in the family to hang up a coat or sweatshirt, and to hook their backpacks and bags onto. For our family that meant at least eight pegs.

2. Put a large basket in the corner of the mudroom for people to kick off their shoes into. We also put down a heavy-duty plastic tray to hold muddy or wet shoes so they wouldn't ruin the floor.

3. Set up a bench so people had a horizontal space if they needed to unload things from their book bags or lay things out for the next day.

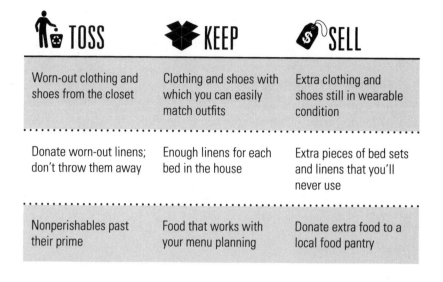

🗑 TOSS	📦 KEEP	🏷 SELL
Worn-out clothing and shoes from the closet	Clothing and shoes with which you can easily match outfits	Extra clothing and shoes still in wearable condition
Donate worn-out linens; don't throw them away	Enough linens for each bed in the house	Extra pieces of bed sets and linens that you'll never use
Nonperishables past their prime	Food that works with your menu planning	Donate extra food to a local food pantry

See if any of these approaches will work for you in your mudroom. I'll admit that ours doesn't always look 100 percent perfect, but it's a lot better than it used to be. More importantly the mudroom is functioning exactly how we envisioned it would work for us.

Total Cash Back in This Chapter

Who knows what kinds of treasures you'll find when you finally get around to clearing out the clutter in your closets, pantry, and mudroom? Maybe you'll get lucky like Jennifer did—finding all of these unwanted gifts that she ended up selling for $1,000 on eBay. Even if you get just 1 percent of that for each unwanted item you uncover, that's better than having things taking up space and collecting dust when they could be bringing in cash.

Total Cash Back in This Chapter: **as much as** **$1,000**

chapter 9

GETTING YOUR HOME OFFICE UNDER CONTROL

I've tried many ways to get my home office organized. I've spent money on rolling carts that could hold hanging files. I've invested in desktop bins to hold my papers. But the problem was always this: No matter what organization system I'd set up, I never took the time to file my papers and put them where they belonged.

Along with my lazy filing habits, there was another problem: I started and stopped so many different organizational systems over time that I never quite knew where to actually put a piece of paper. Was I using the vertical file system this week or the desktop bin one? Had I cleared out a drawer in my cabinet for filing, or was I using file boxes to keep my papers organized?

Bottom line: I always ended up with a paper-covered desk, swearing that I knew where everything was in the mess, but usually spending way too much time looking for things that should have been at my fingertips.

Steps to Clean Off Your Desk

The second Monday of January is National Clean Off Your Desk Day. However, there's no reason for you to wait until this actual date to start tackling the mess in your home office—whether you have an actual desktop, you work on a table, or you have piled so much paper around the room that you can't see your work space anymore. Here are some steps you can take to get your desk cleared off so that you can actually use it to get work done—and then how clearing it off can save you some money.

IDENTIFY PAPER TO KEEP, RECYCLE, OR SHRED

As you start going through the paper on your desk, on the floor around your desk, or wherever you like to pile paper, keep this in mind: You need to decide with each piece of paper one of three things. Will you:

O **Keep it to file:** Paper you keep to file is anything important that you need for work or home. This could be a contract for a job or receipts you need to keep for this year's tax returns.

O **Reuse or recycle it:** Paper you'll reuse or recycle falls into one of two categories. Paper that has been used on both sides—and doesn't contain any sensitive personal information (credit card numbers, social security information)—should go into your recycle bin. Paper that is printed on one side only and is still in good enough shape to be reused, should be set aside to use in your printer. It's a good idea to get in the habit of printing on both sides of a piece of paper before tossing it in the recycle bin, because this will save you money in the long run. Case in point: Before I started using this trick, I was buying a case of paper every six months. These days, because I reuse paper by printing on both sides, I buy a case of paper every nine to twelve months. The difference is worthwhile because a case of paper costs about $40.

O **Shred it:** Paper you'll shred includes the aforementioned paper with sensitive information on it. You don't want to risk your personal security or increase chances for identify theft by just recycling this paper in your regular recycle bin.

FIND OTHER OFFICE SUPPLIES THAT YOU CAN REUSE

Keep in mind that as you go through stuff, it's great to be able to recycle items. However, it's even better to keep them out of the waste stream—and save yourself some bucks from having to buy new—by reusing whatever you can.

So, for example, when I was trying to get my desk in order and came across manila envelopes that the school had used to send home communications, I put them aside. Then I stored them in my filing cabinet drawer where I keep office supplies. The idea here is that I would reuse them (with new mailing/address labels, of course) the next time I needed to send something. This saved me from having to buy envelopes for a little while.

Getting a Shredder on the Cheap

Cross-cut shredders, the kind that chop paper into little bits, are the best kind to own. They quite literally reduce any printed information that you don't want to share with prying eyes into pieces of confetti. Unfortunately, these shredders also can be expensive.

To get a shredder on the cheap, peruse your local Freecycle group or Craigslist ads, where you might find one for free or at least at a discount. You can also check in with your local school district or a nearby college or university. Schools often have equipment sales that allow you to find furnishings for a home office at significant savings. Finally, if all else fails, take advantage of any Black Friday–like sales to get a new shredder. Two years ago I did this, and was able to get a shredder that normally retails for a couple hundred dollars for about $80.

THIN YOUR MAGAZINE AND NEWSPAPER COLLECTIONS—FOR MONEY!

Are you a newspaper and magazine junkie like I am? Then chances are you probably have piles of magazines all over your house that you plan to catch up on sometime in the near future—something I discussed in Chapter 2. Well, guess what? The future's here. And if it's been three to six months since you picked up that latest issue and you still haven't read it, you never will. With my extra magazines, I give away overruns on Freecycle or bring to my local doctor's office for the waiting room. Or I find ways to reuse them around the house, as I mentioned in Chapter 2.

Also, you should make a note of the magazines that you subscribe to or buy on the newsstand on a regular basis but *never read*. How much money are you wasting with these subscriptions or purchases? Accept that your time is limited and stop spending money on stuff that just ends up in a pile anyway.

At one point I was doing more than just picking up the newest issue of a design magazine while I was in line for groceries: For many years I collected vintage magazines—with the hopes that, one day, I would turn those magazines into decorative items for my house. On rare occasions I did frame old-fashioned advertisements and hang them up, or I used these magazine images to decoupage something. But I was buying magazines at garage sales (even for a few pennies a piece) and cluttering my home with them.

Finally, I decided I needed to get rid of those piles of magazines and maybe recoup some of my investment in them. Maybe you need to do the same? The good news is that, eventually, I made a few dollars selling them on eBay and Craigslist, and by consigning them to a local thrift store. The bad news? I hardly made back what I'd spent over the years. But at least I had a little extra cash in my pocket and a lot more space in my home office.

The Power of Neat Piles

One day I had an epiphany about home-office organization. I'd visited a colleague who was going to be showing me how to use some new website tools and had invited me to work with him, along with some of our other colleagues, in his home office.

Like me this person had a lot of paper on his desk. But unlike the usual state of my home office, his desk did not seem to be cluttered at all. Why was that? Because he'd organized his piles of paper so that they didn't scream "clutter" or "disorganization." Instead, those piles looked neat and orderly.

I know that organizing clutter seems like a contradiction, but hear me out. Here's what this person had done:

1. First, he'd grouped like documents together.

2. Next, he'd placed each of the piles in a clearly labeled file folder.

3. Then, he'd laid out the piles in three neat rows on his desk, one overlapping the other just so, much like a game of solitaire.

In a single glance, he could see everything he was working on and where it was on his desk. Once everyone had settled in around his desk, he calmly reached for the folder related to our project—easily slipping it out from the folders it was in between—and then pushed the remained folders together to close up the space he'd just created. In no time, we got to work on the tutorial. This ingenious way of organizing clutter inspired me to tackle my own messy desk.

It took me a while to work my way through my clutter, but these days if you walk into my office you'll see a line of fanned-out piles of paper that represent everything I'm working on at that moment. Sure, I've still got a few piles I need to work through—mostly in the form of books—but I'll take care of that problem once I get around to putting up some shelves on my bare office walls.

Here are some ways that you can start to get your desktop organized with the fanned-out folder system.

GET YOUR FILES STARTED

You don't have to spend money on new files. I'll bet that if you rummage through your file cabinets or look in your supply closet, you'll find lots of file folders that you can reuse, or boxes of new folders you forgot you owned.

If you can't find the folders that you need, you can always swap with a friend—maybe she has more file folders than she knows what to do with, and you have an overflow of the hanging folders that she needs. Or you can put a call out on Freecycle to see if anyone has old file folders that they're giving away.

Never thought about reusing file folders? Don't worry if it's already labeled. You can always peel off the old label or put a new label over the old one. Or you can just turn the file folder inside out and, voilà, brand new folder.

CLEARLY LABEL YOUR FILES

Having neatly labeled files will help you figure out where your stuff belongs. How you define "neatly labeled" is entirely up to you. You can handwrite your labels, use pretty stickers or—if you think having professionally printed file-folder labels will inspire you to stay organized—then go ahead and invest in a label maker.

If you choose this latter option, please make yourself this promise: If your label maker runs out of batteries or tape, you will not put off replacing those batteries or tape. Here's why that's an important promise to make to yourself. When you do procrastinate about getting those necessary supplies, it means that you can't make any labels for your file folders. And the longer you go without making labels for your files, the faster your desk and entire home office is going to revert to its disorganized ways.

In other words, don't set up perfectionist roadblocks for yourself that will keep you from turning your home office into a clutter-free zone.

Updating Equipment to Minimize Technology Overload

You may be wondering why I'm suggesting that you buy new office equipment when you have perfectly good office equipment that you can use right now. Well, have you ever calculated the upkeep of each of those machines? If not, it can be an eye-opening experience.

For example, if you popped into my home office last year, along with my MacBook laptop, you would have found the following:

O Color inkjet printer

O Color inkjet printer, copier, and scanner

O Black-and-white laser printer

O Desktop copier

O Fax machine

Sounds like I was all set from a printing, copying, and scanning perspective, right? Well, yes and no. Sure, I had all the technology I needed to make color and black-and-white copies, to scan documents and photographs, send photos, and print out e-mails and manuscripts. But there were two reasons that this setup didn't benefit me from an organizational and financial point of view; I spent:

1. A lot of time switching back and forth between pieces of equipment, depending on the task I needed to complete

2. A lot of money buying supplies for each printer, copier, fax machine, and all-in-one machine

So not only was having a lot of equipment sucking up my time, it was sucking up my money, too.

While a handful of the machines I was using came free with a past purchase of a computer, they were each expensive to maintain. Here's a cost rundown of some of them:

○ **Color inkjet printer and printer/scanner/copier:**
replacement cartridges cost about $35 each—a
color cartridge and a black-and-white cartridge were
necessary for both—and needed to be replaced every
three months

○ **Copy machine:** toner drum/cartridge cost $100 to
replace. I needed to buy a new one every other year

○ **Laser printer:** laser cartridge cost $80 to replace; it ran
out of toner about once a year.

Oh, and did I mention that each of these machines took different print cartridges? So it wasn't like I could stockpile any one kind of ink, laser printer, or toner cartridge when it was on sale and then use it in all my machines. No, I had to buy them all separately.

Needless to say, in the course of the year, I was spending about $300 just to keep up my ink supply. Who wants to spend that kind of money, especially if this way of working isn't time efficient? And then there's the desktop clutter of having so many machines.

That's why this past year I decided to streamline my office machines into one: I got a high-efficiency desktop printer that's also a copier (color and black and white), scanner, and fax machine. I bought it on Black Friday and spent less for it than I did all of last year buying ink. Now if I need to replace ink, I only have to spend once but I still get the functionality of my four-in-one. So far, I'm still on the three-month ink replacement schedule but, like I said, I only have to buy one set of ink cartridges ($60 for both). That means that instead of spending $300 a year on ink, I'm spending $240, saving myself $60 annually.

My plan this year is to sell those machines for extra cash—either on Craigslist or Gazelle.com (*www.gazelle.com*). If none of that works out, I'll donate them to a nonprofit and take the tax write-off—assuming my accountant says that's kosher.

If you think that streamlining your office machines makes sense, wait for a Black Friday deal like I did or for a store promotion in which the store recycles your old machine for you *and* gives you money off your new purchase. For example, at this writing

Quick Clutter Challenge

Think you need to go out and buy new pens? Think about how many pens you may have purchased as back-to-school supplies for your kids or brought home as freebies from a hotel stay. By gathering them all up now, you won't have to spend money later because you think you've run out of pens. A dozen store-brand pens at an office-supply store will set you back $8. That's not a lot of money, to be sure, but why spend it if you don't have to?

For this chapter's Quick Clutter Challenge, set a timer for fifteen minutes, and then see how many pens you can gather up and bring back to your home office. If I were doing this challenge, I would check in my nightstand, the bottom of my suitcases, and under cushions of the couch. You know where your pens might be hiding, so give yourself the chance to declutter and save money! Timer on? Then, ready, set, go!

Staples had this trade-in deal going: If you brought in your old printer, the store would recycle it for free (the store normally charges $10 to recycle an old machine) *and* give you $50 off the purchase of a new printer costing $199 or more. All told, you would be saving $60.

Cashing In
Tory, Washington, DC

We decided to upgrade our TomTom GPS after owning it for two years. I felt kind of guilty having spent the money, so I figured I would recoup some of my costs by selling the old TomTom GPS on Craigslist. I listed it for $40 but after a few days and lots of scam e-mails, I pulled the ad. I thought that perhaps I could donate the GPS to a worthy cause—I'd donated used cell phones in the past to charity—or at least get someone to recycle it. I didn't want it sitting around my house if I wasn't using it but also I didn't want it ending up in a landfill.

Eventually, I discovered Gazelle.com, which gives you cash for working electronics. Gazelle.com has a questionnaire that you complete online so they can see if your electronic device is worth sending to them for cash. They ask questions like "Does it still work?" and "Do you still have all the cords and software that came with the device?" I answered the questions, and then Gazelle.com used the facts to estimate the market value and make an offer for my TomTom: $31. That sounded good to me. Even better, Gazelle.com paid for me to ship it to them. All I had to do was print a shipping label, box up the GPS, take it to the UPS store, and wait to hear that my package had arrived.

Two days later, Gazelle.com let me know via e-mail that they'd received my GPS and were evaluating it. Then two days after that, I got another e-mail telling me that the GPS had checked out and they were mailing me a check for $31.

Gazelle.com will even take my old laptop computer off my hands, but first I need to get four years of pictures off of the hard drive. Then I can ship it and wait for my check.

The Home-Office Deduction

One of the ways that you can make money from your home office is by making sure that you take the home-office deduction on your taxes, if you legitimately work from home. According to the Internal Revenue Service (IRS), you can deduct expenses related to the business use of part of your home if you use it exclusively and regularly to conduct your business or meet with clients, patients, and others with whom you do business. You must also use this regularly defined space for business only. It is important to figure out what percentage of your home's total square footage your home office is so you can use that percentage to figure out how much of your household expenses you can deduct.

Here is the example the IRS uses in Publication 587 on the "Claiming the Home Office Deduction" page of the IRS website (*www.irs.gov*):

Your office is 240 square feet (12 feet × 20 feet).
Your home is 1,200 square feet.
Your office is 20 percent (240 of 1,200) of the total area
    of your home.
Your business percentage is 20 percent.

TOSS	KEEP	SELL
Paper that is damaged or frayed and would jam a printer if you tried to use it, or if it contains sensitive, personal information; then shred it	Paper printed on one side only to reuse in printer	Paper or old school supplies that are still brand new and no one in your house needs anymore
Recycle rather than toss a printer that no longer works, especially if you can get money back for doing so	All-in-one printer	Office equipment you no longer need, such as a stand-alone fax if your all-in-one printer includes a fax machine, too
Magazines older than a month or newspapers older than a week	A month's worth of magazines that you haven't read yet	Vintage magazines that an antiques store or consignment shop might find interesting

This means, for example, that you can claim 20 percent of what you spend annually on electricity as a home-office expense. As far as computers, equipment, and furniture go, if you use them more than 50 percent of the time for your business, they will qualify for a home-office deduction, but in certain instances you have to depreciate the value over time—meaning you can't just write off the total cost of a new desk or computer.

Note: This is just a summary of some of the qualifications for the home-office deduction that you should be aware of. This is not about getting cash for any clutter but rather as a way of making sure you're getting all the cash back possible for any legitimate business expenses you may incur within the confines of your home office. Nonetheless, don't take my advice as gospel. Instead, speak with your tax professional to find out for sure whether or not this applies to you and your home-office situation.

Total Cash Back in This Chapter

Hopefully by the time you've worked through the organizational and clutter-busting tasks in this chapter, you'll end up with a much neater-looking home office. Working in a clean environment can be inspiring and energizing. Once you get a taste of what it's like not to have to be pushing piles aside just to find a space on your desk, you are more likely to want to keep up your habits. And, hey, it doesn't hurt that by getting your home office to be more streamlined, you put some cash back in your pocket.

In this chapter I shared how you can minimize the ink you have to buy for your machine ($60) and snag yourself a discount on a new all-in-one printer ($60). Also, I explained how you can make good money from your old office equipment ($100). Savings as small as the cost of pens or as big as an affordable shredder will start to add up as you get your office in order. And to top it all off, we've uncovered some decent money that you can funnel back into your household budget or sock away in the bank for a rainy day. Plus, don't forget about checking out sites like Gazelle.com and other sites that will buy back working electronics for cash.

Total Cash Back in This Chapter: **$284**

chapter 10

SELLING YOUR STUFF FOR CASH

When I first starting selling my used stuff, I focused exclusively on eBay. One of the site's benefits was that you can search completed transactions and see what similar items actually sold for. This always helped me to price what I was selling. But in the last few years, traditional e-commerce websites started offering free shipping, and buyers on eBay began to expect the same.

If you've ever sold on eBay, you know that one of the ways to make a bigger profit on what you were selling was to slightly mark up your shipping costs. Also, if you weren't diligent about weighing your items before you listed them, you might have ended up undercharging for shipping (something I did often) and losing money on the transaction.

As if the scourge of free shipping wasn't bad enough, eBay instilled limits on what sellers could charge for shipping. At that point, it just fell out of favor as a way for me to make some money from stuff I didn't need anymore.

That's why in this chapter on selling your stuff for cash, I'm mentioning eBay, but I'm not giving it a lot of face time. While I still see eBay as an affordable way to buy items from time to time, I believe that if you're looking to get the most bang for your buck, you should stick with other resale options, such as yard sales, Craigslist, and consignment shops.

Planning a Successful Yard Sale

Most people start out trying to make money by having a yard sale. I know that when I was growing up, my mother could count on getting some decent dollars from a Saturday afternoon spent selling her stuff. But my mother was wicked competitive with her pricing, and it helped that we lived on the corner of a busy road—the drive-by traffic was priceless.

I tried to take a page from my mother's yard-sale playbook once I bought a house and found myself with things I no longer needed, but my yard sales were never as successful as hers were. Even banding together with my neighbors and having a neighborhood yard sale didn't improve things much for us. But I know two things we did wrong. We priced items too high (what can I say? I was being greedy) and we lived in a low-visibility location. Our neighborhood was tucked away in a hillside and was a bad place to have a good garage sale.

Maybe you've tried to have a yard sale, too, but were not successful. Well, here are some suggestions to try the next time:

O   Make yourself more visible. If this means putting out signs, placing ads in the newspaper, or grouping yourself with others in a visible location, such as a community center parking lot, do it.

O   Choose a weekend day when people are likely to be driving around, looking for garage sales. If you live in a sports-oriented town and there's a big baseball tournament going on one weekend, don't have your garage sale then. Your target market is likely to all be at the ball fields instead.

O   Price things to move. Yards sales are not high-end auctions. People want a bargain and, remember, you want to clear out your clutter. Sure, you want to make some money, but at the end of the day, you want to have to take back inside as little as possible.

O   Do your prep work ahead of time. Hit the bank for singles and coins the day before your yard sale so you don't waste time figuring out how to make change when someone hands you a twenty-dollar bill. Price things the night before, too, so you can make those decisions thoughtfully and not in a rush on the day of your sale.

O   Be prepared to open up early in the morning. Most serious yard-salers start their day soon after sunup. So if you want to catch the people who are really going to buy, you need to be open for business when they're out shopping.

If all else fails and your neighborhood yard sale isn't successful, even after following this advice, next time you might want to find a third-party location where you can have a yard sale. Many houses of worship, community organizations, and even local businesses have yard sales from time to time where you can buy a spot for a nominal amount ($10 or $20), and then they do all the work for you—providing a table, advertising the event, and bringing in the shoppers. Though it might hurt to pay someone for something you could do for free in your own yard, if you end up getting rid of more stuff and making more cash, it was money well spent. It's not unheard of, by the way, to take in about $400 in ideal yard-sale conditions.

GARAGE SALE SIGNS THAT SING

Jonathon Papsin, founder of Tag Sell It (*www.tagsellit.com*), an online community connecting people with virtual tag sales, has seen all kinds of garage sale signs. "I've seen everything from paper plates with chicken-scratch scribble to more elegantly constructed signs, most likely done by a professional," he says. While you don't have to spend big bucks outsourcing your signs to a print shop, Papsin recommends that you always include the following eight elements in a garage sale sign—if you actually want to get people to show up and shop at your sale:

1. The street address of the sale

2. The time and date of the sale

3. Arrows pointing shoppers in the right direction to get to the sale

4. Big enough lettering so people can read it from far away

5. Keywords on the sign that are likely to catch someone's eye, like "Antiques," "Art," or "Tools"

6. Bright and bold signs and printing that catches people's attention

7. Not so much information that someone driving by can't read your entire sign at thirty miles per hour

8. Signs that are waterproof and windproof, in case Mother Nature doesn't cooperate

Papsin suggests creating multiple versions of your sign and placing them in all high-traffic spots on the way to your sale. He also recommends spreading the word by telling your friends, posting information about the sale on neighborhood and community bulletin boards (both online and offline), and, of course, listing your sale for free on *Tagsellit.com*. (Putting something in Craigslist's "garage sale" section probably wouldn't hurt either.) Finally, Papsin always advises people to take down their signs as soon as the sale is over so they don't clutter the neighborhood and become a nuisance and eyesore.

What's It Worth?

How does $41,000 for a video game sound to you? Sounds pretty great to me, and if you've been a gamer for the past few decades, you might be in luck. It seems that some of Atari and Nintendo's original fans have held onto their old video game consoles and the games themselves from the 1980s and 1990s, and now they are worth big bucks. One person recently sold a Nintendo Entertainment System (the console that plays the game for you) on eBay for $14,000. She thought it was a piece of junk. Turns out it was a gamers' classic find. After that sale, video game lovers nationwide starting scouring their basements for vintage video games, and some turned up gold: One guy found a still shrink-wrapped Nintendo game from 1987, and it fetched that heart-stopping amount mentioned earlier—$41,000.

According to gaming experts, some of the most valuable video games are those from the Nintendo NES, the system that played that $41,000 game. Nintendo stopped making that gaming system in 1995 so if you or anyone you know still has boxes of video games from the 1980s and 1990s, you might want to go through and see if you've got anything of value. By the way, even used NES games get a decent price—a used version of that game that sold for $41,000 also sold at auction but for *only* $1,000!

Bottom line: If you've got a bunch old video games, make sure you do some extensive Internet research on them before putting them out in the fifty-cent bin at your garage sale. Who knows? One of them could get you a down payment on a house!

Getting Cash via Sales on Craigslist

What can I say about Craigslist? I love its versatility, I love that it's free to advertise on, and I love that it's helped to put hundreds of dollars back into my pocket for things I would have just put out on the curb as trash. The trick to successfully selling on Craigslist is to provide as much detail as possible and to include a photograph.

Here are a few examples of situations where I've used Craigslist to get extra cash, and the detailed ads I've used:

SELLING A BATHROOM VANITY

While renovating one of our bathrooms, we pulled out the existing vanity. The cabinets were stock quality with the counter-top attached. I didn't think it was worth anything but figured it couldn't hurt to try selling it on Craigslist.

Before we uninstalled the unit, I photographed it and then uploaded that photo to my Craigslist ad.

Here is the ad I used:

> **Bathroom Vanity (cabinet, countertop, sink, Delta faucet) $25**
> *We are redoing our bathroom and are selling the vanity that no longer works in the new space. This vanity cabinet comes complete with:*
>
> - *off-white marble-like countertop with integrated shell-shaped sink and soap dish*
> - *attached backsplash*

- *Delta faucet*
- *oak cabinet with four drawers and a double door to access plumbing*

The vanity with countertop measures 49 inches wide by 18 inches deep by 31 inches high. The countertop, door faces, and drawers were just cleaned; this vanity is ready to be installed.

I couldn't imagine that someone would want this 1960s vanity, but within a week I had a buyer and $25 in my pocket.

GETTING RID OF A WOODEN FIREPLACE MANTEL

We also renovated our dining room recently. In addition to painting the walls and having the floors refinished, we decided that we wanted to take the fireplace in the dining room back to its natural state. That is, the previous homeowners had painted the brick surround a sky-blue color. We wanted natural brick to be exposed instead. But before we could start removing the paint, we had to remove the mantel.

With the help of a pry bar, I was able to take off the wooden mantel in one piece and then put it up for sale on Craigslist. Again, I made sure to photograph the piece before I'd uninstalled it and included as much description as possible.

Here's the headline I used:

Wooden Fireplace Mantel (Mantle): $40

This wooden fireplace mantel (mantle) was just removed from our dining room, and we would love to see it find a new home. The mantel, which came off in one piece, measures 58 inches wide by 56 inches tall. It has detail work on the front that really makes it stand out from other plain wood mantels. It should be easy to install in another home.

Notice that I spelled "mantel" two different ways. That's because I'd discovered in other Craigslist listings that people spelled it either "el" or "le." Though "mantel" is the proper and

Supporting a Good Cause

It almost goes without saying that if you find yourself with items you can't make money from, don't throw them out—donate them to a good cause. Thrift stores that support houses of worship, domestic violence shelters, hospitals, and other good causes all rely on people's generosity in donating items they no longer want and that they can sell for a profit in their retail stores. So while it's great to get cash in your pocket for your goods, if all else fails, it's even better to help out those who are all about helping others. Plus, if you get a receipt for your donation, you can likely use that as a tax deduction. (Check with your accountant to make sure this applies to your tax situation.)

preferred spelling, I wasn't going to be a spelling stickler if it meant people in the market might skip over my ad because they spelled "mantel" as "mantle."

A guy drove two hours to my home a few days later to pick up the mantel—and paid me $40 for it.

MAKING CRAIGSLIST WORK FOR YOU

In addition to the items above, I've also sold a playground set ($100), a Fisher Price toy box ($20), and a filing cabinet ($10) on Craigslist. If you take away anything from this section of the chapter, it should be this:

1. You can sell nearly anything you want to get rid of on Craigslist.

2. When writing an online ad, include as much detail as possible, such as a full description and dimensions.

3. Always include a photograph. I can tell you from my own experience as a seller and from others who successfully sell stuff online that photos make a difference in how quickly your things sell, and often whether they sell at all. Think about it: Would you have been willing to drive two hours, like the guy who bought my mantel, if you didn't know what it looked like? I did.

I know that some people don't like the having-to-meet-strangers part of selling on Craigslist. I always try to arrange to have a pick-up when my husband is home or someone else can be there with me. Whenever necessary for mutual convenience, I've met my buyer in a safe, public place.

To me, it's worth it for this slight time inconvenience. By selling items this way, I avoid shipping charges and get to keep 100 percent of what I'm making on the sale.

Identify Clothing to Bring to Consignment Shops for Cash

What you need to focus on now is learning what thrift and consignment stores want to see in your castoffs. Why? Well, if you follow their criteria, they are more likely to give you cash upfront for your clothes, or accept your clothing for consignment—which means you'll get paid down the road once they sell your wares.

You should make as much cash from your clutter as possible. For example, the consignment shop I use pays 40 percent of the selling price. Considering that the shop is a bit upscale, with my latest consignment, I stand to make close to $100 on clothing I might have just let linger in my closet. How does $100 extra sound to you right now, especially knowing that your closet is neat and tidy?

Here are some specific steps to follow and tips to take to heart to increase your chances of making money from your clothes when selling them to resale stores and consignment shops.

- ○ **Seasonality.** Don't bother bringing your old shorts and sandals to a resale shop in the middle of October. Unless you live in Florida, it's not bathing suit season anymore, and a thrift store will have no interest in your swimwear. Come back in April or May with those swimsuits, and bingo—you might just make a sale!

○ **Fashionability.** Though Jessica Simpson once appeared on a *People* magazine cover wearing high-waisted jeans, that fashion trend was over in a New York minute. To those in retail, high-waisted jeans are mom jeans, and unless your thrift or consignment shop targets housewives, you should probably just give those out-of-fashion jeans away for free. To make money on denim, they have to have a fashion-forwardness to them, such as a lower rise and a darker wash. I know this because when I've attempted to get rid of my own mom jeans, this low-rise, darker-wash information is the feedback I've gotten time and time again. (Note to self: Buy lower-rise jeans from now on to increase future resale potential.)

○ **Brand recognition.** Many thrift and consignment shops have guidelines that spell out exactly what brands sell well in their stores. One shop where I bring my clothes explains that they'll take anything from Gap to Gucci, but lest you think Isaac Mizrahi from Target fits in this range, the guidelines tell you otherwise. (This store is not interested in mass-market merchandise.) The teen-oriented shop where my daughters sell their clothes says straight out what their three As of consigning are: Abercrombie, Aeropostale, and American Eagle.

○ **Fresh Smelling.** I think it goes without saying that no one wants to buy a stinky piece of used clothing. Even someone shopping at a yard sale would want a garment that's freshly laundered. Stores in the resale sector are no different. Don't want to pay to dry clean something that's dry-clean-only? Then at least give it a couple of good spritzes with Febreze to make it smell fresh.

○ **Cleanliness.** Along with a garment that smells good, you want a garment that looks good, too. Resale shops are going to want articles of clothing without stains. Heck, even sellers on eBay know better than to parade a piece of stained clothing as perfect, lest they get negative feedback. (If you have something that you think is saleable, but it's stained, try my stain-removal trick on page 209.)

○ **Prep It Properly.** Your clothing will seem much more attractive if it's not wrinkled or missing buttons. Take the time to prep your clothes for sale by ironing shirts to a crisp finish, replacing any missing buttons, zipping up zippers so that jackets and pants fold nicely, and trimming off any loose threads or pilling on sweaters so they look neat and tidy.

○ **Appropriateness.** Take a walk through the resale shops where you want to sell your goods and make sure that your own clothing matches what's on the rack. For example, a thrift store stocked to the gills with hunting gear and outdoor clothing really won't want your peep-toe shoes. And you'll never get away trying to consign something from a women's store in a resale shop that targets teens. (Remember those three As?)

○ **Volume.** My local consignment shop makes it clear
   that they won't make a consignment deal with anyone
   unless they have ten saleable items to offer. Because
   the owner is picky—hey, she knows her customers—
   she usually rejects about 50 percent of what I bring in.
   I've learned to bring in much more than I think she'll
   take because I find that the more items I present for
   consideration, the more she takes overall.

○ **Diversity.** Here's a little nugget that you may not
   know about resale shops: Many are interested in
   selling more than just clothing. I've been in thrift and
   consignment shops that sell jewelry, scarves, belts,
   handbags, shoes, books, CDs, DVDs, hair accessories,
   and more. So as you're clearing out the clutter in your
   closet, see if you can't locate non-clothing items that
   you can toss in for consignment consideration.

○ **Package properly.** Make sure you follow the store's
   rules on how they want the clothing delivered. Some
   consignment shops want you to bring in your items
   already on hangers or shoes still in the box. The shop
   I deal with locally wants everything neatly folded in
   shopping bags. Don't ruin your chances of reselling
   your clothing by using hangers when they don't want
   them or bringing in folded clothes when they want
   them on hangers.

○ **Honor Hours of Operation.** The teen store where my
   kids make extra cash from their clothing has a simple rule
   about the hours they take consignments—it's any time

Stain-Removal Trick

These steps should help you get a stain out of nearly anything. Wet the fabric where the stain is, then pour liquid laundry detergent to saturate the stain. Sprinkle on borax powder, and make a paste of the liquid laundry detergent and borax. Let that paste sit overnight, and then wash and dry as normal. If this combination can't get the stain out, that stain will never come out, and you'll just have to take that piece of clothing off your "to-be-sold" list.

during business hours except for the hour before the store closes. Other consignment shops may designate days of the week or specific hours of the day when they'll take clothing to consider reselling. Some require you to make an appointment. Be clear on these hours of operation before you head out to make a consignment.

O **Pick-up Time.** Most consignment shops will agree to sell your stuff for a limited amount of time—usually sixty to ninety days. You should get a contract that says this specifically. At the end of that period, make sure you return to the store to pick up any unsold items. Shops will usually donate the clothes that don't sell. If you think you might be able to take your unsold clothes to another resale shop to make money, don't let this "donate date" pass you by or you'll miss out on an additional chance to bring in cash for your unwanted clothing.

USING A MIDDLEMAN

If you think it's worth it and you don't mind paying a little extra to reach a larger audience, maybe using a store that sells people's stuff on their behalf via eBay is the right move for you. With names like iSoldit, these stores are usually in regular strip malls and work with tech-phobic or time-starved pack rats. Prepare to hand over up to 40 percent of what the store makes on your sale (that's no different than what a consignment shop takes).

One person I spoke to made $135 on a camera that a shop in North Texas called EasySale sold for her, and even 40 percent of $135 is more than you'd make with your stuff still sitting in your basement or garage. Some people swear by these shops, because they take better pictures than you can with your cell phone, they have selling track records, and they know how to word the ads to get results. You know what? If I'd exhausted all of my options and I still wanted to try to make some extra cash, I might even give these shops a try.

Cashing In
Dee Dee, Pennsylvania

I have established a relationship with a woman who owns a quirky shop just around the corner from my home. This vintage shop features punk-rock clothing for babies, costumes, collectibles, trendy, vintage, and pre-worn fashions, and the owner's hand-blown glass creations. It's an eclectic assortment of merchandise. One day the idea came to me to ask her if she ever consigned items. She was open to the idea, so the next day I brought her a big Rubbermaid container of costumes and vintage clothing I had been storing for years in my attic. She offered to give me 50 percent of whatever she sold.

At first I didn't know if I would make a cent. My motivation was to clean out nearly thirty years of stuff we had collected. Our house has very little storage, and the boxes of costumes, toys, clothing—and let's face it, junk—were starting to overwhelm me.

When I open a closet and find something that I just don't need or want anymore, I just put it in a bag and walk it to the shop. I try to get the things out of the house as soon as I decide they need to go so that I don't change my mind. I have to work hard to keep my hoarding tendencies under control.

Thanks to this shop, I've sold a wig I wore in a play when I was in high school (forty years ago), a black satin cape I made for my daughter's witch costume (probably eighteen years ago), an antique black satin and velvet gown in very bad shape, more costumes and vintage clothing, handbags, T-shirts, sweaters, and denim. I think I've made about $250 in the past year. I'm delighted to get anything for things that I really want out of my life and not have to throw them out.

Where to Consign Clothing

There are probably thousands of individually owned resale, thrift, and consignment shops, or events where you can get some cash for your clothing clutter. I would recommend doing a Google search to see what you can turn up locally, or using the website of NARTS, the National Association of Resale Professionals (*www .narts.org*), as a resource. On the site's Shopping Guide page, you can search by state, zip code, or merchandise category for nearby resale stores.

In addition to locally owned stores, there are also national events and store chains that work on a consignment basis to help you make money from your closet castoffs. Here's a handful worth investigating.

BUFFALO EXCHANGE

Although it sounds like an upstate New York restaurant or a Bob Marley song knockoff, Buffalo Exchange (*www.buffalo exchange.com*) is a fashion-forward thrift store that buys clothing for men and women. The store recommends that you call your

Quick Clutter Challenge

If you've got kids, then you've probably got toys. And games. And books. Chances are your kids' playroom is cluttered with things they have grown out of. Well, guess what? Instead of collecting dust, you could be collecting some cold, hard cash for them. So here's a Quick Clutter Challenge. Set your timer for fifteen minutes, and head into the playroom or your kids' bedrooms. Find things that you know they're just too old for, are still in good condition, and don't hold any sentimental value (you don't want to sell stuff if it would hurt your kids' feelings). You can probably find enough toys to consign the next time you bring clothes to a kid-oriented consignment shop.

local location before coming in, because employees can tell you what they're most in the market for and what they're not interested in reviewing. This will save both of you the time and aggravation of having your stuff rejected. (And trust me, it's hard not to take these rejections personally. Even though you want to get rid of the things, you simply don't want to hear "We're not interested in this piece.") So be prepared: Buffalo Exchange will tell you on the spot which pieces they want, and how much they will offer for them.

Additionally, if you're in a shopping mood, you can negotiate a trade so your new purchases could end up being free. As of this writing, you'll find Buffalo Exchange stores in fourteen states, including New York but, no, they're not in Buffalo—Brooklyn and Manhattan only.

CHILDREN'S ORCHARD

The one benefit to bringing your kids' gently used clothing and other goods to the Children's Orchard (*www.childrensorchard.com*) is that they take off-season items throughout the year. That means that should you clean out a closet in June and find the snowsuit your son grew out of, the Children's Orchard would still be happy to take it off your hands.

Like other resale shops, the Children's Orchard gives you cash upfront, but they offer special terms that can up the ante: If you're willing to take a store credit instead of cash-in-hand, they'll give you even more for the items you're selling to them. I guess if you're still buying for young kids, this is a good deal. Sure, it doesn't put actual greenbacks in your pocket, but it does help take

Quick Clutter Challenge

Most people think about selling their regular clothes at consignment shops, but many places also take accessories. For this Quick Clutter Challenge, hunt down scarves, belts, handbags, jewelry, and other accessories that may have some resale value. So set your timer for fifteen minutes, and see how many items you can find in the accessories category that you can consign for cash, too. Ready, set, go!

the sting out of buying things in the future for your kids. You can find store locations in twenty-four states.

JUST BETWEEN FRIENDS (JBF)

The JBF twice-a-year shopping event (*www.jbfsale.com*) offers people like us the chance to set up our own consignment shop "booth" to sell children's clothing, maternity wear, and other kid-oriented products in an established space. These consignment events occur in places ranging from convention centers to houses of worship to fairgrounds. You split your profits with the JBF franchise owner that organized the sale. Even with the commission cost, most moms I spoke to say that they still take home enough cash to have made this worth their time. Plus, they don't have the stress of organizing their own yard sale.

Once you register with JBF, you have access to their pricing software, which allows you to print out professional-looking price tags. As of this writing, there are JBF consignment sales occurring in twenty-two states, from Arizona to Wisconsin.

ONCE UPON A CHILD

This national chain (*www.onceuponachild.com*) buys pretty much anything having to do with babies and young children—gently used clothing, strollers, furniture, toys, and more. Some parents I've talked to reported only getting about a buck an item for their kids' clothing, and about $50 for four pieces of kids' furniture. They were not happy about this and thought they should have gotten more for their things. Only you can decide if this kind of money is worth it to you or if you'd rather take your chances having a yard sale. You'd do best to bring in a volume of items to sell, and make sure you check the brands list and quality/condition guidelines on the website before trekking to the store.

Also, because of recent recommendations from the Consumer Products Safety Commission (CPSC), Once Upon a Child will only take items that have not been recalled due to safety hazards. So if they reject a car seat or a game, which you think is in perfect condition, it's likely because they are looking for only safe things to resell. Therefore, it's a good idea to check online at the CPSC website at *www.cpsc.gov* before trying to sell your kids' cast-off clothing or toys. Once Upon a Child currently has locations in forty states and three Canadian provinces.

PLATO'S CLOSET

This national chain of resale stores (*www.platoscloset.com*) focuses on clothing and accessories that fashion-forward teens and tweens (kids ages ten to twelve) would like. Unlike traditional consignment shops that pay you once they've sold your things, Plato's Closet gives you cash upfront and on the spot—well, after they've had some time to review your clothing. On a busy day this can take a couple of hours, so get ready to wait. Know that they are ultra picky about the items they take. Be sure to check out the Most Wanted page on the Plato's Closet website before you arrive so you can identify brands that do well there.

🗑 TOSS	📦 KEEP	🏷 SELL
Stained, torn, or worn-out kids' clothing	Clothing your kids may grow into	Children's, tween, or teen clothing that's still in good condition
Books that are missing pages or written in (recycle them, please)	Books you still enjoy	Popular books that still have value
Adult clothing that is stained, torn, or worn-out	Your own clothing that you still have in rotation	Designer label or recognizable brands that are still in fashion and wearable, but which you no longer want
Costume jewelry that's broken or missing pieces (try giving away on Freecycle first, unless it's made of gold)	Jewelry and accessories you love and wear regularly	Gold jewelry you no longer want and/or fashionable jewelry that has resale value

You'd do even better to bring in a lot of your middle schooler's or high schooler's castoffs so that you'll at least come home with enough money to have justified the trip. Volume is the way to go here. Expect to get $2 to $3 per item—at least that's been my experience. However, I know a woman who once got $15 for a pair of Hollister jeans that she'd only worn twice.

Plato's Closet also takes clothing, shoes, books, CDs, jewelry, and bags for both boys and girls. As of this writing, you'll find Plato's Closet locations in forty-three states as well as Ontario and Saskatchewan, Canada.

Cash Back in This Chapter

At this point you should have all the information you need to sell your stuff and make extra money from items you might have just tossed out with the trash. You also have detailed instructions on making your Craigslist ads sing to potential buyers, plus tips on getting your clothing ready to bring to a resale shop. All told, you should have no trouble thinning your stuff and making extra bucks, too.

Total Cash Back in This Chapter: **$745**

chapter 11

GETTING WHAT YOU WANT BY SWAPPING OR TRADING

I hope that by now you have a better sense of what it takes to make cash from your clutter. However, as I've shown in some of the earlier Toss, Keep, Sell charts, there are times when you can't actually sell something that you want to get rid of. So, instead of keeping it as clutter or throwing it out, your best bet may be to trade it for something else.

This chapter focuses on how you can stay true to your decluttering mission, but instead of making money from your excess stuff, you can swap or trade it for something else you need. Don't give away stuff just to get stuff that will create more clutter. Instead, let's look at the various categories where swapping or trading makes the most sense.

Swapping for Books

For the longest time I donated my books to the library or Goodwill when I was done with them. I still like to do that, but first I try to save myself some money by swapping my old books for new ones.

I decided to start looking for alternate ways to get new books to read when I looked at my annual book spending. As I mentioned earlier in the book, I used to spend $800 a year on books. Why lay out that kind of cash when I could figure out ways to get the books I want and need for practically free?

In doing some research, I found out that there are a number of online swap sites that focus on books. One kind of swap site is set up for a one-for-one swap. That means that if you have J.D. Salinger's classic *The Catcher in the Rye* and want Jennifer Weiner's *Good in Bed*, you need to find someone who is giving away a copy of *Good in Bed* and wants *The Catcher in the Rye*. Personally, I think that's too much work and relies too much on luck. I'd rather work with swap sites that give you points for each book you agree to give away and then let you cash in those points in the future to get the books you want. Sites like this include PaperBackSwap (*www.paperbackswap.com*) and BookMooch (*www.bookmooch.com*).

Here's what I've grown to love about swapping books: It thins my book collection so that my living room, bedroom, and home office all look less cluttered, since they're the rooms with the most bookshelves in them; and it saves me money. Sure, I have to spend money to send books to someone who wants to swap

Swap Sites to Check Out

For books and movies, the best swap sites, as far as I can tell, include:

- O Bookins (*www.bookins.com*)
- O BookMooch (*www.bookmooch.com*)
- O PaperBackSwap (*www.paperbackswap.com*)
- O SwapaDVD (*www.swapadvd.com*)
- O Swaptree (*www.swaptree.com*).

Many of these sites let you swap video games as well so you can thin out and refresh several collections at once!

with me, but it's a nominal amount—maybe $2.50 per book. In the year or more that I've been swapping, I think I've spent $50 total on postage, but the value of books I've received for free far exceeds that amount.

I'll admit that there is no guarantee that you can get the book you want in a timely manner via a swap site. However, coupling it with a renewed interest in borrowing books from the library will help to guarantee that books will never again take over your space and that you won't spend crazy amounts of money on books you can find for free.

After going through your book shelf, you could go from crazy cluttered to clutter-free!

Swapping for Movies and Music

We're not one of those families that collect movies like souvenir pins. Sure, we have all the Disney classics—on VHS, no less—and a few movie favorites that the kids like to take on car trips for entertainment. But other than that, we do not have a problem with DVD spending. We're the same with music. We have our favorite CDs from way back when, and will download music from time to time, but we're not obsessed with it.

The best way I can explain the benefits of swapping DVDs and CDs as a way of decluttering and saving money is through the story of a woman named Kam whom I once interviewed. I met her while researching an article on—no surprise—swapping.

Kam is a movie lover. She and her husband got into the habit, many years ago, of buying new releases as soon as they came out, and over time collected more than 1,000 DVDs. She had always justified these purchases because she doesn't pay for premium cable and because her busy work schedule never allowed her to be home when the library was open—where she could borrow movies for free.

Kam is also a big reader like I am and a music lover. During our interview, she guessed she may have had nearly as many books and CDs as she did DVDs. With the economy sliding downwards, Kam realized that she was going to have to rein in her movie-buying ways. One day when she and her husband went out looking for new furniture to add bookshelf space to house their media collection, it dawned on Kam: Maybe instead of *buying* bookshelves, she should start *selling* the DVDs, books, and CDs she owned.

Kam tried eBay at first and that didn't work so well. Then she stumbled on swapping sites. Those, on the other hand, worked *very* well for her. She estimates that in the past year, she's given away two hundred DVDs, one hundred books, and three hundred CDs, but she's benefitted in two ways:

○ She still saw one hundred new movies in a year because of the old DVDs she's swapped for new ones.

○ She has made between $4,000 and $10,000 in the value of the media she no longer needs and can swap in the future when she's jonesing for a movie, book, or CD. (She calculated this figure after subtracting the amount she spent shipping media to other people. Still a pretty impressive amount though!)

Oh, there's one last benefit: With her media collection thinned, Kam actually sold some of the bookcases in her home for cash on Craigslist. That had her coming out ahead even more.

 ## Cashing In
Jason, California

I grew up in the '80s and have a zillion CDs. I didn't think they were worth anything, because I knew that if I took them to the record store down the street, they would offer me pennies. Then I read an article about how to "get rich slowly" by selling off stuff like old CDs. I was surprised to learn that people will buy used CDs online.

I ended up listing about one hundred and fifty CDs on Amazon Marketplace and got a minimum $5 per CD. On some CDs I made even more.

I priced things by checking around the Amazon Marketplace and seeing how other people were pricing the same CDs I wanted to sell. In one instance I happened to have a Pet Shop Boys EP that I paid $3.99 for originally—it still had the price tag on it—and I noticed that other sellers on Amazon Marketplace were listing it for close to $100. I figured it was valuable, and it was: I ended up selling it for $57. Turns out there are a lot of CDs like that: For whatever reason the record company didn't print a lot so now they're considered to be rare and can fetch more money.

What I like about dealing with Amazon Marketplace is that, unlike eBay, where you have to write the listings yourself, on Amazon Marketplace all you need to do is enter in the CD's SKU number, and it pulls up all the information automatically. It's important to have the jewel case and insert not only for the SKU number but also because that's what people want when buying a CD. Then they know it's not a counterfeit copy or a CD you burned yourself.

This has worked out really well for me, and I've probably made about $300 on CDs so far.

LEAH'S OWN QUICK CLUTTER CHALLENGE

Jason's story inspired me to go on my own Quick Clutter Challenge in my basement—where we have two file boxes filled with CDs. After sifting through a couple of piles, I pulled out three old CDs that I thought might be worth something.

One was a 10,000 Maniacs album, *MTV Unplugged* from 1993 that was packaged in a handmade paper, bright pink envelope instead of a jewel case. It was sold in conjunction with the Body Shop in a limited quantity—25,000 copies only. Well, I guess it wasn't a big seller, because you can find hundreds of copies for sale online for a mere $4 each. (I think I paid $12 for the CD way back when.)

The second CD I found said "limited edition" right on the cover. It was a music sampler from BMG Distribution, also from 1993, and said "For promotional use only." BMG must have handed out hundreds of thousands of these so-called limited edition CDs, because they're all over Amazon Marketplace for about a buck a pop.

The final CD was the one that ended up having some value, to my surprise. It was a still shrink-wrapped CD from singer Aaliyah. It was her album *I Care 4 U*, which came out in 2002 and which I got as a giveaway at a party. What makes this CD potentially valuable? Aaliyah died in a plane crash in 2001 so this was, in fact, her last CD. When I checked out the CD on Amazon's Marketplace, I found it selling for as much as $25—and the seller had that CD listed as being "like new." Mine is, in fact, new, having never been opened. This has me wondering how much I could possibly get for it.

Knowing this, are you ready to see if you've got valuable CDs somewhere in your house? If so, get your timer ready and go find some CDs to sell.

Swapping for Kids' Stuff

In my day, swapping kids' clothing was called hand-me-downs, and I gladly accepted them from any family member or friend who was willing to offload any clothes, toys, or kid gear that they'd grown out of or no longer needed. These days not everyone has family or friends with kids the same age or they don't live close enough to meet easily, which is why swapping for kids' stuff has become so popular.

It's also a money saver, to be sure. I'm not surprised that cash-strapped parents are looking for creative ways to get the stuff they need for their family without spending extra cash doing so.

As far as getting your home organized and cutting down on kid clutter, getting involved in swaps is a no-brainer. This is something you can do via your house of worship, the preschool your kids attend, a neighborhood association, or even Craigslist.

Lots of parents swear by swapping sites as well. This takes the pressure off of them to deal with people they know—in case they are somewhat embarrassed that they are giving away and getting stuff for free; for some there is still some stigma attached to wearing what I call hand-me-downs.

Quick Clutter Challenge

Swapping DVDs and CDs is a great way to stay entertained while clearing out your clutter. For this Quick Clutter Challenge, set your timer for fifteen minutes and see how many DVDs you can locate that you can swap. Don't give away your kids' favorite movies, and remember that swapping sites aren't interested in DVDs that are missing their original containers. But if your *American Pie, American Idiot,* or even American Girl days are over, why not grab those disks and see if you can't swap them for something you do want. Set your timer, and go get your DVD and CD clutter!

From my research I found that the best site for swapping kids' stuff is Zwaggle. Unlike many swap sites that give you a point for each item you're willing to swap, Zwaggle (*www.zwaggle.com*) lets you assign a value to your item using "zoints" (what the site calls points). So you might say that a stroller you want to "sell" for the equivalent of $50 is worth fifty zoints.

The nice thing about Zwaggle is they'll give you twenty-five zoints upfront when you join, as opposed to other swap sites where you have to give away five or ten items before you earn anything you can trade with. You continue to earn more zoints as you give stuff away. As far as the stuff you can give and get on Zwaggle, it runs the gamut. I've heard of parents swapping the normal stuff, like diaper bags and dresses. But from time to time you'll find stuff like musical instruments and favors for a baby shower.

Like most swapping sites, the giver pays shipping. According to Zwaggle users, the site's Fed Ex shipping tool makes that much easier on the sender's part. I don't know if it's necessarily cheaper than sending something via US Postal Service or UPS, but it's definitely more convenient.

Finding Swap Sites

While I've provided a few examples of swap sites I know and use, they may not be the right swap sites for you. Maybe you don't like the interface or the variety of products doesn't fit with what you're hoping to give away or get in return.

Also, swap sites can come and go like fly-by-night businesses. A few that I'd researched for a swapping story I wrote recently for *Good Housekeeping* magazine were gone, *finito*, shut down by the time the story got to the fact-checking stage. That's why I would recommend that if you decide to start swapping, start asking around for sites that people you know use and trust. Don't have any friends nearby who are swapping? Well, maybe one of your Facebook friends can suggest a place for you to check out.

Bottom line: Always do your homework on swapping sites before you spend the time taking pictures of your stuff and before you ship anything. Remember super-swapper Kam? The site she first started using when she started swapping went out of business one day after she'd earned enough points to get a free Xbox. Well, when Kam went to redeem her points for that new gaming system, all she found was an Error 404 message on the web page where the swapping site used to be.

How to Organize a Swap Event

A lot of people like the notion of swapping but don't like the impersonal nature of swap sites. For these folks who want to give away their old stuff, get new things to take home, and enjoy face time with friends, a swap event is the perfect answer. And organizing a swap event isn't as hard as you might think.

For example, if you want to have a clothing swap, you don't have to stress out about inviting same-sized women only. Believe it or not, clothing swaps that welcome women of all shapes and sizes are the ones that people tell me are the best attended and received.

Think you want to organize a swap get together? Here are the steps to take.

PICK YOUR LOCATION

Most clothing swaps occur in people's homes. It provides the intimacy of a small get together, and people can slip into the powder room when they need to try on something. However, there are other places where you can hold a swap.

○ **Your office.** A friend of mine who works in a real estate office organized one after hours at work. She booked the conference room (windowless, of course) and brought in refreshments for people to enjoy while they shopped and swapped.

○ **A thrift shop or other kind of clothing store.** For a small fee, a retail shop may agree to host your clothing swap and offer your attendees a discount on merchandise on the racks. Sure, this kind of kills the notion of a free swap, but it does open up some opportunities for people who want to attend a swap for social reasons but don't like the idea of shopping for clothes in someone's house.

○ **A house of worship or community center.** You may find everything you need to throw your swap party in one of these locations—a big meeting room, plentiful bathrooms, and probably even a kitchen if you want to cook up some snacks to serve.

YOUR GUIDELINES

Swap organizers recommend having set guidelines so that people know what they can bring and what they should leave at home.

Some swaps are specific to clothing and accessories only. Others allow people to bring household items along with books.

The only problem with expanding the boundaries of your swap beyond your original idea is that it makes it more difficult for people to find even exchanges. I would recommend starting with a clothing swap, with the understanding that people can bring anything that's related to clothing—shoes, scarves, belts, and bags. Then you can assign a value that makes sense for everyone. For example, a pair of pants is worth two accessories, or something like that.

You might also want to give out dot stickers by color to each participant. That way your friends can tag what they're giving away and keep track of their stuff as people claim it.

The other guideline you should communicate to your group is simple courtesy: Make sure that anything they're bringing to swap is clean (or at least fresh smelling) and in good enough condition that someone could wear it home. Stained, torn, and worn-out clothes should go into a rag bin, not a "to be swapped" bin.

FINALIZE THE DETAILS

O **Set a date and time.** If you're inviting all moms, then having your swap meet during the day—when kiddies are likely in school—will help you to draw the most people. If your friends work, then clearly an evening or weekend date would be better. Give yourself at least two hours for the swap event so no one feels rushed during the swap.

○ **Encourage presentation.** If possible provide somewhere for people to present what they're willing to swap. Tables are a given, and if you can get your hands on a rolling rack or something else where people can hang their clothing, that's even better. If you want people to hang their stuff up, be sure to inform them to bring their own hangers.

○ **Provide space for changing.** Even the closest of friends may not want to be stripping down to their underwear in front of each other. Make sure your guests have access to a bathroom or powder room as a makeshift dressing room. At the very least have a couple of full-length mirrors so people can check out how they look in their soon-to-be new clothes and accessories.

○ **Arrange to donate unwanted clothes.** Regardless of how much great stuff people bring, there is always going to be some clothing left over that no one wants. Rather than burden your guests with having to take their un-swapped items home, arrange it so that the next day you or one of your swap participants can make a trip to Goodwill or another place where you can donate those clothes.

Free Appraisal Days

Think you have something valuable that's worthy of being auctioned off? Then why not bring it in to your local art gallery or auction house on the next free appraisal day? These usually occur on a regular basis, because, as Jeff Jeffers of Garth Auctioneers explains, though people know they may have something valuable in their house, they often wait for these free appraisal days for motivation to get their item appraised. I find that interesting, since you never pay a fee to have an appraisal done on any other day of the month; the only catch is you've got to make an appointment ahead of time for the appraisal.

If this sounds like something you'd like to try, do a Google search using the term "free appraisal day," and you're bound to get millions of hits. Add in the name of the town or city where you live, or the kinds of items you're hoping to get appraised, and you'll get even more targeted results that will help you locate a place near you where you can bring your potential treasures.

For example, friends of ours gave us a Roseville pottery dish for our wedding. I have no intentions of selling it, because I love it and use it regularly for serving dinner. But I know that Roseville can be considered a collectible, and I've always wondered what the dish is worth. If I were interested in getting it appraised, a Google search helped me to figure out that near where I live, there is actually an auction house that specializes in Roseville pottery—and has a free appraisal day once a month!

The only downside to free appraisal days is that they are often crowded and busy. Jeffers says that on the last Tuesday of the month, when his business does free appraisals en masse, he has three employees working for eight hours straight on a line of people that stretches out the door and around the building.

TOSS	KEEP	SELL
Books with broken bindings, missing pages or covers, or that you've written in	Books you plan to read in the near future	Swap books that are still in near-perfect condition
DVDs that are broken, cracked, or scratched	DVDs that are still family favorites or classics you could watch again and again	DVDs that still play well, are movies you no longer wish to watch, and you have the original case
CDs that are broken, cracked, or scratched, or are missing the original jewel case	CDs of your favorite bands	Any CDs that still play perfectly. Whether or not you need the original jewel case and the insert that comes with it varies by swap site.
Baby clothes that are stained beyond repair. Turn them into rags and save the money on paper towels	Baby clothes that have sentimental value	Swap clothing from well-known labels like Gymboree and Baby Gap
Car seats that were in a car accident, and/or strollers or playpens that have been recalled	Baby equipment that may serve a purpose	Sell or swap baby gear in great or perfect condition
Same as kids' clothes: anything worn, torn, stained, or out of fashion, make it a rag	Clothing you've worn in the past six months or know you'll be wearing next season	Clothing still in good-enough-to-wear condition and still looks current

234

Total Cash Back in This Chapter

The interesting thing about swapping is that it fits this book's mission of helping you to clear out your clutter, but it doesn't necessarily get you cash in return—in the traditional sense. That's because swapping is all about a made-up currency. You can give and get valuable items with no money changing hands, but as you can see from my own example with books and Kam's example with movies, swapping can add up to a lot of money saved over a single year.

Total Cash Back in This Chapter: **$5,000** to **$10,000** a year

ABOUT SUDDENLY FRUGAL

Suddenly Frugal (*www.suddenlyfrugal.com*) is the blog I started in 2007 when my family and I needed to create a roadmap for better living within our means. We'd just sold our old house to pay off home-equity debt, and we swore we'd never allow ourselves to get in such a hole again. Thus, our Suddenly Frugal lifestyle.

Since 2007 I have been posting on my blog nearly every business day. Along the way I've garnered tens of thousands of regular readers and some regular features that people come to expect and definitely enjoy. By far the most popular posts are the ones that have to do with free stuff, which is why my regular Freebie Friday post (on Fridays, natch) drives a lot of traffic to my blog.

In addition to sharing money-saving ideas on Suddenly Frugal, I also share money-*earning* opportunities, such as how collecting loose change around your house can put extra money in your pockets. (You'll see this is advice I share in *Toss, Keep, Sell!*) I've added up my spare change in lots of different ways—from hours spent rolling coins and to dumping a big bowl of change into a Coinstar machine during a promotion when Coinstar was giving you extra money back, just for using their machine. (I wish they'd do that more often, as those Coinstar machines are so convenient.) In response to these posts, Suddenly Frugal readers have replied via comments with their own money-making tips. In the case of spare change, they let me and everyone else know that some banks and credit unions have their own coin-counting machines that don't charge you a fee for using them. That's pretty cool.

I've also road-tested tips and ideas on Suddenly Frugal before adding them to this book, such as how to prep your clothing to improve your chances at a consignment shop and how to organize a yard sale that brings you big bucks. I did the same with the content of my book *Suddenly Frugal*—road tested it, that is. However, like *Suddenly Frugal*, I haven't just taken copy from my blog and pasted it into *Toss, Keep, Sell!* Most of the information you'll find in both of my frugal-living books is original.

Why am I telling you all of this? Because I hope that after reading *Toss, Keep, Sell!* you'll sign up to receive my blog posts by e-mail (I used Google's Feedburner for this free service for my readers), and if you don't already own a copy, you'll pick up a copy of *Suddenly Frugal* as well.

APPENDIX A

I've grouped together in one place the website addresses for the companies, products, and stores that I've mentioned in *Toss, Keep, Sell!*

1-800-GOT JUNK junk removal service
www.1800gotjunk.com

Amazon Marketplace
www.amazon.com

Antiques Roadshow TV show
www.pbs.org/wgbh/roadshow

Book Mooch book swapping site
www.bookmooch.com

Buffalo Exchange resale store
www.buffaloexchange.com

Children's Orchard
www.childrensorchard.com

Coinstar coin-counting machines
www.coinstar.com

Consumer Product Safety Commission
www.cpsc.gov

Craigslist
www.craigslist.org

Easy Sale eBay Consignment store
www.easysale.net

eBay
www.ebay.com

Facebook
www.facebook.com

Febreze fabric and air freshener
www.febreze.com

FreeCycle Network
www.freecycle.org

Garth's Auctioneers and
Appraisers
www.garths.com

Gazelle.com (where to sell
used electronics)
www.gazelle.com

I Sold It on eBay
www.877isoldit.com

Just Between Friends Sale
www.jbfsale.com

National Association of Resale
Professionals, organization for
thrift and resale shops
www.narts.org

Once Upon a Child
www.onceuponachild.com

Paper Back Swap
www.paperbackswap.com

Plato's Closet, resale shop
geared towards tweens and
teens
www.platoscloset.com

Replacements Ltd., buyer and
seller of old and new china,
crystal, and silver
www.replacements.com

Rubbermaid storage
containers
www.rubbermaid.com

Staples office supply store
www.staples.com

Tag Sell It (community of tag
sale enthusiasts)
www.tagsellit.com

Zwaggle
www.zwaggle.com

APPENDIX B

I've offered many different ways that you can get every room in your home organized, and in some instances I suggest actions to take along the way. Both to reiterate those actions and to better explain why they're relevant to the *Toss, Keep, Sell!* mission, I have included more details on certain things you can do along the way towards getting cash for your clutter—or just getting your clutter out of the house.

Check Your Spices

Like anything else that you might use to make a meal, spices have an expiration date. That's the bad news. The good news is that expired spices won't make you sick like, say, expired milk, but they also won't flavor your meal in ways that you expect. In other words they may add *no* flavor to your meal. And then where are you with your recipe? You can pinch spices and then do a sniff test—knowing that if they give off no recognizable odor whatsoever, they're done for. Or, you can use the "How Old Are Your Spices?" tool on the McCormick website (*www.mccormick.com*), which will help you to determine if spices are long past their prime or if you can keep them around for a little longer. Of course, I realize that this tool could be seen as a gimmick just to get you to buy new spices—McCormick is one of the largest spice-making companies around—but as someone who does a lot of cooking with spices, I see the value in knowing if my tarragon should be in the trash instead of in my spice cabinet.

Dispose of Old Medications in a Safe Way

Probably the worst thing you could do when dealing with old paint or medicine is to flush it down the toilet. Studies nationwide have shown that traces of everything from antihistamines to Zoloft are showing up in our water supplies. Sure, this can be traced to people who actually taking these medicines, um, excreting them, but it's more likely the result of lazy disposal of old meds. Therefore, when you begin to declutter your bathroom and find old bottles and boxes of medications that are past their prime, don't flush or toss them without considering these options first.

○   Mix the medication with coffee grounds, seal them in a container, and toss with your regular trash. (Don't recycle.)

○   Ask your local pharmacist if he or she can take back expired medications and make sure they are disposed of in a safe manner.

○   Make a note of when there is a drug take back day, such as the one that the Drug Enforcement Agency (DEA) hosted nationwide this past fall. Most drug stores and municipal buildings were open for a single day for no-questions-asked taking back and disposing of prescription drugs. (Read about the details of this program on the DEA's website: *www.dea.gov.*)

Donate Towels, Linens, and Sheets to Animal Shelters

Animal shelters, humane societies, and other good causes that care for abandoned animals have an endless need for linens of all kinds. They use these donated goods in a variety of ways, including towels to dry off animals after they've been bathed and sheets to line pens so that the animals can rest on a soft surface. Turns out there are other items that you may find when decluttering that animal shelters will gladly take from you, such as old newspapers, blankets, and plastic bags.

Look for Recalled Toys and Children's Furniture

Here's how the U.S. Consumer Product Safety Commission's website (*www.cpsc.gov*) describes this government agency's mission:

"The U.S. Consumer Product Safety Commission is charged with protecting the public from unreasonable risks of serious injury or death from thousands of types of consumer products under the agency's jurisdiction. The CPSC is committed to protecting consumers and families from products that pose a fire, electrical, chemical, or mechanical hazard or can injure children. The CPSC's work to ensure the safety of consumer products—such as toys, cribs, power tools, cigarette lighters, and household chemicals—contributed significantly to the 30 percent decline in the rate of deaths and injuries associated with consumer products over the past 30 years."

243

As far as you're concerned, if you're looking to sell old toys, children's furniture, or any other consumer "product," it would be well worth your time to search the recalled-products section of CPSC website before trying to bring anything to a resale or consignment shop. These shops are responsible for keeping dangerous products out of their stores and will likely reject upfront anything they deem as having been recalled. So why waste your time getting all those things together, in hopes of making money from them, when they should just end up in the trash anyway.

Recycle Plastic Bags

As far as the environment and your budget is concerned, you'll do best to bring reusable bags with you when you go shopping—especially if you're shopping at store, such as Target, which gives you money back for bringing your own bag. That said, I understand that there are times when taking a plastic bag is your only option. Or maybe you've stockpiled them, like I used to do for all of my future dog walking. When it comes time to get rid of those plastic bags, as part of your decluttering, it's best to recycle them in one of the bins you might see outside of supermarket. Bags in these bins are either recycled into other plastic bags or turned into plastic-based decking materials, such as the kind that Trex makes. Check the Plastic Bag Recycling website at *www.plasticbagrecycling.org* to find a store near you that collects plastic bags for recycling.

INDEX

About the Author

Leah Ingram is the creator of the nationally syndicated blog called Suddenly Frugal (*www.suddenlyfrugal.com*), and an expert on how families can live more meaningfully on less. She is also the author of fourteen books, including *Suddenly Frugal: How to Live Happier and Healthier for Less* (Adams Media, 2010), *Gifts Anytime! How to Find the Perfect Present for Any Occasion* (ASJA Press/iUniverse, 2005), *The Everything® Etiquette Book, 2nd Edition: A Modern-Day Guide to Good Manners* (Adams Media, 2005), and *Tie the Knot on a Shoestring* (Alpha Books, 2007).

In addition, Leah has written hundreds of newspaper, magazine, and website articles on nearly every topic under the sun, including back-to-school savings (*Woman's Day*), planning a wedding that benefits a good cause (*Parade*), and using eBay to shop for prom bargains (*USA Weekend*).

In 2006, a profile she wrote about breast cancer survivors for *Triumph*, an American Cancer Society magazine, received two custom-publishing awards. They were an APEX Award of Excellence for Interviewing and Personal Profiles and a Magnum Opus Silver Medal in Writing.

Leah has appeared on television hundreds of times to discuss family-related topics, including gift tips, etiquette advice, and shopping suggestions. She's been an expert guest on *The CBS Evening News with Katie Couric*, *Good Morning America*, CNBC's *Market Wrap*, *BusinessWeek* TV, *ABC News Now*, and *Good Day New York*, among other programs. In addition, she's acted as a media spokesperson for many national brands, including Bank of America, T-Mobile, and Starbucks.

Leah is a graduate of New York University, with a bachelor of arts in journalism, and the Protocol School of Washington, where she received her certification as an etiquette and protocol consultant. She also trained in TV hosting at TVI Actors Studio in New York City. She lives in New Hope, Pennsylvania, with her husband, two daughters, and faithful canine companion and walking partner, Buff.